LIA LEENDERTZ

THE TWILIGHT GARDENER

A GUIDE TO EVENING PLANTING AND ENJOYING THE GOLDEN HOURS

PAVILION

CONTENTS

Introduction 4

The Nocturnal Gardener 8

Dealing with the Practicalities 10

PART 1

MAKING YOUR TWILIGHT GARDEN A REALITY 12

Planning and Design 14

What's your Night-time Garden Style? 16

Organising Space 26

Using Colour 28

Using Scent 34

Using Lighting 38

Using Water 44

PART 2

ENJOYING YOUR TWILIGHT GARDEN 46

Making the Most of your Twilight Garden 48
At Home Bonfire Night with Sparklers 54
Star- or Moon-gazing Party 56
Camping in the Garden 60
Theatre Night in the Garden 64
Summer Barbecue 66
Wildlife in the Night-time Garden 70

PART 3

PLANTS AND PLANTING 76

Star Plants 78
Supporting Cast 128
Backstage Beauties 180

Index 220
Picture Credits and About the Author 223

Introduction

When we picture our ideal garden, we mostly think of sunny days and of a garden filled with flowers, butterflies and light. But if you only ever spend time in your garden in the bright light of day you are missing some of its most charming moments: the twilight hours when moths flit between pale flowers in the gloaming; the darkening night when candles are lit and the night-scented flowers reach their headiest; the deepest velvet times, when the stars start to sparkle. Our gardens are our havens, our peace in a busy and frightening world, and this is even more true in the evening, when they become safe and cosy refuges in which to enjoy the qualities of the night.

This book has been written to help you unlock the potential of your garden at dusk, to make it welcoming and beautiful with evening planting, lighting ideas and design tips that work perfectly well in the day and come to life at night. With this book in your hand, I hope you will find your own ways to make more of your outdoor space, at a time when it is usually neglected. In doing so, I hope you will find magic.

There are so many possibilities in the evening garden. You might just want a secret hideaway, a place to relax on your own with your senses fully attuned as you smell the sultry fragrances of night-blooming flowers and listen to the scuttling of nocturnal creatures and the trickle of water. If you have children, you may be used to a garden filled with activity: of brightly coloured plastic kid's toys that ring to the sound of laughter, and tears, and demands for drinks and snacks. How gorgeous to reclaim it in the hours after you have ushered them into baths and pyjamas. In a cramped family home, a garden designed for night-time can be a breathing space, and a place to reclaim your exhausted self and let your shoulders drop. A few candles, your favourite drink and a rocking chair set within a pretty, scented garden are all you need.

RIGHT: The White Garden at Sissinghurst Castle Garden, Kent, England, is the ultimate model for an evening garden.

The night-time garden isn't all about peace and quiet though – once you have made your garden alluring for the evenings you may well find yourself inviting people into it. In Part 2, discover why moving any gathering outdoors makes it a special event, taking ourselves out of the everyday and into something otherworldly. This book will show you how to turn the garden into everything from a candlelit, outdoor dining room, where the fresh air acts as a digestif, sharpening the appetite and making all foods taste extra delicious; into a garden theatre; a night-time observatory; or even a fairy lit campsite, with the only decoration the pale blooms of borders filled with plants chosen for their ability to glow in low light.

Hedgehogs, moths, bats and glow-worms all come out at night, and are among those creatures that need all the help we can give them as they struggle with habitat loss and climate change. In this book we will not only discuss how to make your garden a welcoming place for others but also for nocturnal wildlife, much of which only moves around at night when hidden from prying eyes. You will also learn how to track and watch them while they go about their lives, almost entirely obliviously.

An essential part of the garden is flowers, and a large section of this book is dedicated to them. This feels like a secret only for those in the know, but there are great swathes of flowers that only release their scent at night, while most are is indoors. These are often the paler flowers that glow in dusk light, their scent and paleness attracting night pollinators that would not find them otherwise. When combined with the backdrop planting that I will suggest in Part 3, and the design tips to help pool and gather scent, these plants will make your garden into a fragrant haven that truly comes alive at night.

There is every chance that up to this point you have overlooked the glorious potential of your garden in the evening – as a space for gathering, for wildlife, or just for you. Most of us do. I hope that within these pages you will find inspiration to change that, and to make your garden beautiful at this most enchanting time.

Lia Leendertz

LEFT: Design your garden so that it lures you outside in the evening.

The Nocturnal Gardener

It is easy to imagine that the daylight hours are the best time to be in the garden, and to shut the door on the whole place as soon as night starts to fall, but a garden is special in half-light and even more special in moonlight or candlelight. While some plants recede into darkness, others leap out in the gloaming. Purples and blues that can be gloomy in the day become pinpricks of vibrant colour, while white – which in the middle of a sunny day can be blinding – glows, gently, at dusk.

Night gardening is necessarily a sensuous experience: as you rely less on sight, the other senses come into play. Many scents actually become stronger at night, and we are perhaps more likely to notice them because our sense of sight has become blunted. In addition, the sound of trickling or splashing water travels further in the still of the night, as do the sounds of any visitors to your garden.

These visitors include wildlife. If you can be still and quiet, you may find yourself surrounded by the snufflings of hedgehogs and the flutterings of moths. If you are really lucky, you might spot a bat swooping by or hear owls and foxes going about their business.

But it isn't just a question of luck. There is much you can do to make your garden more attractive to night-time wildlife; for example, by having plants that are attractive to night-flying insects and through sensitive, organic garden management.

All these things can make your garden a more exciting place to spend time in at night. If you really get it right, you might even get a glow-worm or two to light up the end of your garden.

In this book, I explore all the different aspects involved in creating a night-time garden – from how to plan your space around your personal needs, to the mood you are trying to create, the colours to use, the best ways to attract wildlife and, finally, how to put all of those aspects together to make your garden a place you are drawn to evening after evening.

Dealing with the Practicalities

Having decided how you want to use your garden and what features you are going to include, you are ready to make a start on the practicalities. Few of us have the good fortune to start with a blank canvas, so the first step is to look at the plants and hard landscaping features that are already in your garden and think about what you want to keep and what you really can't live with. It is always simpler to work around existing features.

Put particular thought into keeping as many of the existing larger plants as possible. Ripping everything out and starting again may be satisfying, but you will lose any sense of maturity in the garden and you will also create more work for yourself. Sometimes just clearing away around an old tree or shrub or doing a little judicious pruning can bring out a wonderful shape and character that you never knew it had before, so examine each plant for possibilities.

The next step is to measure out the available space and make a scale plan of your garden on graph paper. Include all of the garden's features that you intend to keep and mark the aspect on the plan – whether the garden is north-facing, west-facing, and so forth – as this will affect your choice of plants. Next, add in the new features you want to include. Cut out paper versions of them to scale and play around with them on the plan until you come up with something you're happy with.

Now you are finally ready to put any new hard landscaping in place – paths, patios, pergolas and arbours. There are many night-scented climbing plants to choose from, so try to include as many structures for them to clamber over as you possibly can.

Next, after any major landscaping has been carried out, comes the new planting. Again, you may want to make a plan on paper before you start planting. As a quick rule of thumb, put any structural planting in first – hedges, topiary, trees and shrubs – and then 'fill in' with the other, more ephemeral, plants.

You will be keen to get on with creating your garden, whatever the time of year, but there are certain jobs that really should be done at particular times for the best results. Structural planting is really an autumn and winter job. These plants need masses of soil preparation to benefit from getting their roots into the ground during cool and wet times of the year. More ephemeral planting can be done at other times, but you will find yourself doing a huge amount of watering if you plant at the height of summer, so try to avoid this.

ABOVE: It is always simpler to put paths and seating areas into place first, then plant around them.

PART ONE

MAKING YOUR TWILIGHT GARDEN A REALITY

PLANNING AND DESIGN

The planting, of course, is the exciting part of any garden. It is really the main ingredient of a beautiful twilight garden, although it isn't the only one. Before you put in a single plant, take some time to think through the way you are going to use your outdoor space and how much time you actually have to maintain it – each type of garden has different needs in terms of hard landscaping, lighting, storage and even planting.

So, is yours a front or a back garden? Is it going to be family-oriented? Is it going to be a calm, relaxing, solitary space where you can go to unwind at the end of the day?

If you are planning on a family garden, you might want to include a lawn, a sandpit or other play equipment, a washing line, and some storage to put the children's toys away when they're not using them. If you think you're going to use your garden for entertaining, you'll need a decent-sized deck or patio. If you're more of a gourmet, then it might make sense to invest in a good, solid outdoor kitchen, and to make your table setting the focus of the garden. If you are planning on spending quiet time alone in the garden, you might want to think about comfortable seating and some large, screening plants to make you feel tucked away and private.

Another consideration is whether you want to spend lots of time pottering and tending your plants or whether a low-maintenance garden, filled with shrubs and other plants that require little care once they are established, would suit you and your lifestyle better.

ABOVE: Don't neglect front gardens. Scented plants such as Rosa 'Helenae' will be a treat to come home to.

What's your Night-time Garden Style?

Look in detail at some of the different ways you might use your garden and therefore what features you might consider, or concentrate on, for each plot type. One of these night-time gardens is bound to be the space of your dreams.

FRONT GARDENS

Imagine walking down the street of an evening, perhaps on your way out for a meal or on your way home from a late night at work. Suddenly you're enveloped in a cloud of intoxicating scent. You look around and spot a garden gleaming with pale flowers. That's where the scent is coming from. It is the sort of garden that you would make a small detour to walk past, one that would lift your spirits when you came across it.

The front garden is a hugely neglected space. All we do is walk through it when going from the house to the street and vice versa, and that's why people rarely expend any energy gardening in it. But it is also an area that sees a large amount of traffic and there may be many passers-by, particularly in the evenings as neighbours return from work and evening revellers head out.

I always feel that a well-designed and cared-for front garden is a community-spirited thing. You may not be out there at night very often, but passers-by will appreciate any work you put in, particularly if you fill your front garden with night-scented plants that perfume the street. And a beautiful front garden will help beautify the area, too, perhaps even inspiring neighbouring gardeners to create their own terrific spaces.

As I have said, the practicalities of a front garden are all about getting from the house to the street and vice versa as quickly as possible. To achieve this, you need a good, smooth path. You can have a pathway that meanders around pretty plantings, but chances are that the postperson will find the shortest route to your front door, even if it means leapfrogging over a garden wall. This means that a straight path from street to door is usually the best option.

FEATURES IN FRONT GARDENS

You should also consider the lighting in your front garden. If you are near streetlights, you may get away without having any extra lighting, but if you're in a darker corner, you may want to consider installing a motion-sensitive light that switches on when you walk up the path. That way, you can find the keyhole even after an evening out. Alternatively, you could install some bollard lights along the pathway.

Making the most of your night-time front garden also means thinking about people you rarely consider – for example, the couple walking home who enjoy the air filled with the smell of night-scented stock, or the late-night dog-walkers who stop to admire your glowing lilies.

Choose scented climbers such as honeysuckle (see pp. 94–95) to clamber around your front door or, of course the queen of all climbers, Japanese Wisteria (see pp. 96–97). Line your path with pale-flowered, night scented shrubs such as *Philadelphus*, which lives up to its common name 'mock orange' (see pp. 154–155), and use *hydrangea arborescens* 'Annabelle' for drama (see pp. 172–173).

You can add beauty to the night-time street scene all year round—consider plants such as jasmine (see pp. 98–99 and 124–125) and winter honeysuckle (see pp. 178–179) for winter scents.

ABOVE: Motion-sensor lights are a stylish and sustainable way to keep front gardens accessible during the evening hours.

TINY BACK GARDENS AND BALCONIES

If you only have a tiny scrap of a back garden or a balcony – perhaps just space for a couple of chairs – you might think it's impossible to have an idyllic night-time garden. However, in some ways a balcony-sized patch makes the perfect space, particularly if you are short on time. For a start, it can be relatively easy to create privacy on a balcony. Pop up a garden parasol, place a couple of larger plants along the front, and you have your own leafy hideaway. Your options are limited to sitting, admiring and sniffing, with perhaps a little plant-tending, but that's not necessarily a bad thing.

In such a small space, detail is everything, so before you start on any plant- or furniture-buying, see if there is anything you can do to improve the look of the floor and walls. Sometimes just a lick of paint on the walls can make a huge difference. Paint them white or cream to reflect light, or terracotta if you prefer a cosier atmosphere.

In a small backyard, consider splashing out on some beautiful paving. You can afford the best as you won't need much of it. Because of the weight of paving, this won't be practical for a balcony, but if your balcony floor is made from ugly concrete, even painting it with a suitable outdoor paint will make it look better.

On a balcony and in a paved backyard, everything will have to be in pots.

Choose a few highly summer-scented plants, such as lilies (see pp. 86–87), *zaluzianskya ovata* (see pp. 112–113), night-scented stock (see pp. 114–115), heliotrope (see pp. 92–93) and *mirabilis jalapa* (see pp. 104–105), and plant each in its own pot. Then intersperse the pots with plenty of box-topiary shapes and big-boned plants such as *cordyline australis* (see pp. 190–191) and *trachycarpus fortunei* (see pp. 192–193), again in individual pots.

Having so many plants in pots will mean lots of watering in summer, but this shouldn't be too hard to keep up with on such a small scale. However, you need to water daily at the height of summer and find someone to water for you if you go away on holiday or for a long weekend. You might want to think about installing a drip-irrigation system to make watering easier. This involves running a hosepipe fitted with drippers through your collection of potted plants, with one dripper per pot. You turn the tap on low and, 15 to 30 minutes later, everything has been watered. When you go away, you can put a timer between the tap and the hose so the water is turned on for a set amount of time each day.

Make sure you leave space among the plants for a couple of chairs and a small table, even if it is only large enough to balance a couple of glasses and a lantern on.

ABOVE: Even a small balcony can offer you all the essential ingredients required for the perfect evening garden.

Try to make use of any walls and ceilings, too – the roof of a pergola makes a good ceiling substitute. Attach hanging baskets full of flowing foliage to the ceiling and baskets full of petunias to walls. Look out for wall-mounted candle holders and lantern-hangers too.

You should also consider a water feature, even in the smallest area. Many, like wall fountains, are essentially just a small water tank and spout. Standing flush with a wall, they take up little space but look magnificent. Choose a classic design in which the water emerges from a lion's mouth into a small pool of water or the contemporary variation, with the water flowing over a sheet of stainless steel or glass, often into a completely invisible reservoir.

Plant lots of green, leafy plants around your wall fountain and, even when it is newly installed, it will look as if it has been there for decades. The gentle trickle of water can provide just the right level of comforting noise to distract you from the sounds of the street below or beyond, and can make your balcony or tiny backyard patch a really special place to be in the evenings.

CONTEMPLATIVE GARDENS

Perhaps you see your garden as a retreat from the world, from people and from noise and bustle; a place where, come evening, you can unwind, perhaps meditate or simply sit quietly in a comfortable chair with a drink by your side. If this vision of a quiet, contemplative twilight appeals to you, there are several things you can put in place to create it.

First, you will want to create a little privacy. This can be hard to come by in the back garden, particularly if you live in a built-up area. The windows of neighbouring houses will often directly overlook the patio or deck where you are sitting. Creating some kind of canopy solves this problem instantly, particularly if it is mainly from above that you are overlooked.

You can put up a sail canopy simply and quickly, and it will instantly make your seating area feel as if it is nestling in its own little world. Bear in mind, though, that a sail canopy can also reduce light levels fairly severely in the house if it is placed too close.

Verandas are paved areas covered by a solid roof, which can be of glass. Verandas provide a good degree of privacy as well as great protection from the rain. Having a veranda means you can enjoy those warm but wet summer evenings as you sit in the dry, listening to the rain patter off the roof when everyone else in the neighbourhood has had to scuttle indoors. It makes the evening feel even more special when you know you're the only one who is out there enjoying it. The only drawback with verandas is that, in some areas, you will you have to seek planning permission to construct one. You will need to check with your local planning authority.

A pergola offers little protection from the rain and doesn't provide as solid a hideaway as a sail canopy, but it is relatively easy to erect, doesn't require planning permission, and lets through plenty of light. Plant yours up with climbing plants such as clematis (see pp. 134-135), honeysuckle (see pp. 94-95) and jasmine (see pp. 98-99 and 124-125), and it will quickly become more private. If the crossbeams of your pergola are placed far apart, string taut wires between them to give the climbing plants something to grow along. They will quickly provide a leafy roof for your seating area.

If privacy from upstairs onlookers isn't an issue, you may want to consider creating several areas for contemplation around the garden. Arbours and seats in the heart of the garden are far from the hustle and bustle of the household and can make perfect places to sit and think. Arbours are particularly good, as they provide some degree of privacy and you can make the most of their vertical surfaces by training night-scented climbers up them.

An area for quiet contemplation will be tricky to achieve if it is constantly assaulted by noise from outside the garden. The sound of vehicles and other comings and goings are difficult to avoid in built-up areas, so instead, concentrate on making your own relaxing noises within the garden to act as a distraction. This doesn't mean playing whale music at loud volume, though.

While you might not think that the gentle trickle of a waterfall could compete with the bleeping of the nearby pelican crossing, this sort of constant, pleasant, low-level noise can be surprisingly effective. Consider installing a small, trickling water feature or, if you want something much easier to set up, you might think about hanging up wind chimes.

Personally, I can't abide tinkly wind chimes, but I'm quite fond of the wooden ones that clap and clank in a low-key, almost maritime fashion. Plants can join in, too. Black bamboo (see pp. 188-189) rustles beautifully in the slightest breeze, and will complement the clanking of wooden wind chimes perfectly. *Nandina domestica* (see pp. 196-197) is known as 'heavenly bamboo', despite not actually being a bamboo at all. Its leaves make a papery, rustling sound.

In a contemplative garden, you will want to keep the lighting low-key: lamps, lanterns and candles are particularly suitable if you are using the space for meditation. You will also want a comfortable set of chairs or even a wicker sofa to lie about on, and you might consider some big Middle Eastern-style cushions for really luxurious lounging. If you opt for these, though, you will also need a large, waterproof storage box or shed to throw them into at the end of the night or if rain threatens.

FAMILY GARDENS

A family garden has to be many things to many people, but if you have a young family and still want to be able to enjoy your garden in the evenings, storage should be high on your list of things to provide.

Large, sturdy storage chests with lids that double as seats are the perfect solution for families that want to be able to hurl all of the children's brightly coloured plastic toys out of sight come evening. You can buy these chests ready-made or have them custom-built in the form of long benches around the edges of a patio or deck. A sandpit with a good-looking wooden cover can also be perched on in the evening; they beat those sandpits with flimsy plastic covers hands down on looks, too. Hammocks are another perfect family-garden feature, providing fun for children and relaxation for adults.

If you use candles or lamps at night in your family garden, they need to be safely installed and out of reach of children, so consider hanging a few lamps from pergolas or buying wall-mounted candle holders. Older children often enjoy joining the adults in the garden in the evenings, and a barbecue or pizza oven is a great way to lure them out and get them interested in cooking outdoors. You can build either a barbecue or a pizza oven relatively cheaply and make it into a permanent feature of the garden, always ready for an evening of outdoor snacking.

Swing seats and hammocks are great choices for family gardens. They make for terrific fun in the daytime and convert to calm, restful and even romantic seats come evening. Large swing seats on frames aren't the most attractive thing, however; instead consider plain wooden swing seats that you could hang from a sturdy pergola or tree.

Lawns are a must in the family garden. Choose a hard-wearing seed mix (often labelled 'Family Lawn', or similar) that contains a high proportion of tough ryegrass. Keep the lawn well maintained to avoid it turning into a muddy mess.

ABOVE: Eating outdoors can bring the family together, creating a fun and relaxed environment.

ABOVE: Cosy, enclosed areas help you feel secure in the garden at night, while also trapping and magnifying the scents of flowers.

Organising Space

Although there are different practicalities to put into place for different types of gardens, there are a few design constants that apply, particularly to a night garden.

Perhaps the most important is creating a sense of enclosure. Many people choose to leave their gardens open to their surroundings, making the most of borrowed views. An open, airy garden can be a lovely thing, but it doesn't make for the ideal night garden. If you want to make the most of night-scented plants, you have to close off the outside world and create a still pool of air where the fragrances will be trapped and will linger and mingle for as long as possible.

A sense of enclosure also helps to create a private, enveloping garden, somewhere you will feel safe and hidden away after dark. Tall, dense hedges comprised of yew (see pp. 218-219) should be your first line of defence. Grown along the boundaries of a garden, they provide a unity of background and create the feeling of a walled, secret garden, even if your garden doesn't have fabulous walls – or any walls at all. Hedges and taller trees planted around the boundaries will also filter much of the wind that attempts to blow away your night-time fragrances. Even in winter, bare tree branches will break the full force of any wind and will make your night-time winter garden a more inviting place to be, if only for ten or fifteen minutes at a time.

Dramatic silhouette plants such as *cordyline australis* (see pp. 190-191) and *trachycarpus fortunei* (see pp. 192-193) also have their place in a night-time garden, whatever its purpose. Position some of these spiky, craggy plants on your garden's boundaries and enjoy the impressive shapes they make against the dwindling light of the evening sky.

Using Colour

As day turns to night, the colours in your garden change. The bright reds, oranges and yellows that are most likely to catch your attention during the day slowly dull and deaden as the light fades. In their place comes – predominantly – white.

All the finest moonlit evening gardens are filled with white, silver and the palest yellow plants. This is common sense: dark colours absorb light rather than reflect it. White, on the other hand, fires every scrap of available light back at us, so the white appears brighter as other colours fade. It is not only gardeners who have noticed this. White flowers are often pollinated by night-flying insects such as moths. These insects use the flowers' night-time glow as well as their scent to help them navigate towards them.

Silver-leaved plants are also effective reflectors of low light. The silvery effect is created by the hundreds of thousands of tiny pale hairs that cover the leaves. These plants generally thrive in full sunlight and hail from hot, Mediterranean climates. Their reflective surfaces have evolved in an attempt to fend off the worst heat of the sun and to help keep the plants cool. These reflective properties work just as well in low light or moonlight, of course, although silver-leaved plants are generally not quite as reflective as white flowers, despite their metallic element.

White leaps out of the gloom and moonlight brings it even more strongly to the foreground. That is why a twilight or evening gardener should consider white their most useful colour and should try to pack in as much of it as possible.

On the other hand, you also need to consider how much you use the garden during the day. Lots of white can be overpowering on a bright sunny day; if your garden includes a mass of white, come midsummer you'll find yourself regularly dazzled. Therefore, if you need your garden to work well in the daytime in the heat, too, it is probably best to use white a little more sparingly. Mix it in among other colours or concentrate on white-flowered climbers used at the back of borders containing other colours. If you garden in a damp climate, though, you may find that the midday-white problem isn't such a big issue. In the dull light of an overcast or rainy day, white can impart the same magical properties as it does in the evening.

RIGHT: Pale-coloured flowers and silvery foliage, such as that of Nepeta 'Six Hills Giant', will reflect low light.

ABOVE: Tulips 'Mount Tacoma', 'Blizzard' and 'White Parrot' in a white border.

OTHER COLOURS

White isn't the only colour that you should consider for your evening garden. Blues and purples, particularly the paler versions of these colours, also tend to leap out of the gloom. Not all blue or purple flowers work, but some, like those of *verbena bonariensis* (see pp. 160–161), seem to have a second life come nightfall. These flowers are perfectly lovely in the day as they bob away on their thin, wiry little stems above the other plants in my borders, but come dusk, it is as if a tiny little light switches on inside each one, and they glow through the twilight.

Even if you mainly use your outdoor space mainly at night, you won't want a garden full of white flowers and silver-leaved plants; you might want to make just a few concessions to daytime viewing. Though it's not for me to advise on your choice of colour scheme.

I don't know if you prefer hot, spicy reds and oranges; cool purples and blues; or even a hotchpotch of all the colours of the rainbow.

What you may want to bear in mind, though, is that white shows up best against a dark background, and that background is often best provided by foliage. So, mix plenty of foliage plants in with your whites and consider backing your evening borders with a dense, deep green hedge. Yew is the densest and darkest of greens, and will throw whites forward. Used as a backdrop, even a privet hedge will serve this purpose well. What you might think of as unattractive in the daytime may not seem so offensive in the twilight.

OVERLEAF: Mix purples, blues and pinks (echinaceas and echinops here) with paler colours, grasses and seed heads to catch evening light.

Using Scent

Planting for a night-time garden is really worthwhile since so many of the plants that look good at night also have delicious night-time fragrances. And one of the attractions of scent is that it's a strong trigger to memory; you may find yourself sitting in your twilight garden remembering your grandparents' honeysuckle-festooned tree or a jasmine-scented holiday evening.

The fragrance of jasmine, evening primrose, lilies and many other night-blooming plants moves up a gear as evening falls. This is all down to those night-time pollinators again (see p. 20). Of course, many flowers that are pollinated by day-flying insects also smell, but in their case, the scent is an added bonus. These flowers rely, primarily, on their looks to make themselves attractive to pollinators. Day-flying insects such as bees and butterflies have keen vision, and it is through sight that they find their sources of nectar. However, night-flying pollinators such as moths and bats have poor vision and low light to contend with, so they depend strongly on their sense of smell. It is usually the fruity or musky scent of the sturdier night-blooming plants that attracts bats, while moths pollinate the smaller, more delicate blooms that have a strong, sweet scent.

Some flowers look good by day or night, but there are others that close during the day and save up all their goodies for nightfall. These plants, such as the Marvel-of-Peru (see pp. 104–5) and night-scented stock (see pp. 114–115), respond to changes in light levels and temperature. They pump certain cells full of water and deflate others to allow their petals to unfurl and emit their scent at nightfall. Come dawn, the opposite occurs, and they seal themselves up firmly to ride the day out.

POSITIONING SCENTED PLANTS

There aren't many rules governing the use of scented plants in the garden. You will probably want to surround your evening seating area with pots of scented plants so you are guaranteed a big hit of fragrance just where you want it most. Lilies, dianthus and brugmansias are among the plants that will grow well in containers, so use these and, if necessary, move them close to wherever you sit in the evenings.

If you have a pergola near your house, you could drape it with jasmine (see pp. 98-99 and 124-125) to make a highly scented evening seating area. Bear in mind, however, that jasmine has a particularly strong smell, so be absolutely sure that you love it before planting. I think the scent is intoxicatingly good, but some people find it unpleasantly overpowering.

Your scented plants don't always have to be up close, however, so don't neglect to put some in the further reaches of the garden. The scents from more distant climbing roses and honeysuckle will drift across the garden and may even be more enjoyable for being slightly elusive. The best bet is to look for opportunities to fit scented plants in everywhere, planting scented shrubs in borders, scented perennials in pots, and scented climbers over walls, trellises and pergolas. Pack in as many as you can throughout your garden, and you'll then get 'hits' of different delicious scents from various points or as you wander around the garden.

OVERLEAF: Concentrate the planting of your scented plants along the edges of paths and close to seating areas to enjoy their fragrance.

ABOVE: Candlelight creates a soft, atmospheric glow, and is lovely when paired with 'warm white' fairy lights of the same hue.

Using Lighting

The phrase 'garden lighting' may conjure up movement-sensor burglar lights that dazzle the entire garden at the twitching of a cat's whiskers, or even an array of uplighters, downlighters and spot lit shrubs that would look more at home in an upmarket hotel garden than that of the average home. The phrase is often off-putting, suggesting complex systems involving trenches for cables and installation by electricians that produce too much light, or the wrong sort of light. Night gardens should be about mystery and magic, and having too much in the way of electric lighting can cause all intrigue go out of the window. How can you appreciate the ghostly outline of a lily in the moonlight if the tree it is next to is bathed in a vivid green glow?

CANDLELIGHT

A little lighting, however, can be a wonderful thing. It can make the night garden more accessible and welcoming, beckoning down pathways and around corners, and it can create magical effects. On an intimate scale, lights on a garden table – candlelight works well because it's beautiful and flattering. Eyes sparkle and skin glows, food looks more delicious, drinks are filled with twinkling bubbles. Everyone is intriguing when their face is lit by candlelight.

Candlelight is easily managed, with a few safety precautions. The best ways to guard against fire risk are to completely contain your flame – which will also prevent it from instantly blowing out the moment there is a breeze – and to never leave it unattended. A storm lamp is a striking way to keep a flickering flame contained outside: essentially, this is a big glass vase into which a pillar candle is lowered. Although they can be expensive, you can also create a budget-friendly version with a big glass jar. One of the beauties of night gardening is that no one can really see how upmarket your candle holder is anyway.

On a smaller scale, empty jam jars make the perfect holders for nightlights, gathered at the centre of a table or placed around the garden. If you have smaller jars, for example baby-food jars lying around, these are also the perfect little holders for tealights. I once saw nightlights used as evening lighting at a country wedding: a couple hundred were spaced along the top of a fence, overlooking a field with hills in the background. The scene was magical as night fell, and I can't imagine that a more beautiful effect could have been created with a lighting budget of thousands. You can also look for vintage containers in secondhand shops that would make beautiful lanterns, particularly those with coloured glass.

FAIRY LIGHTS

Fairy lights have a similar prettiness, and the closest that electric lighting gets to casting the magical glow you get from candlelight. Make sure to choose 'warm white' as cooler tones create a much less lovely effect. If you don't want your garden to look like it is ready for Christmas all year round, use the fairy lights to pick out a pergola, an arch, a tree or around railings (rather than, for instance, draping them over shrubs). 'Bistro lights' are the summery equivalent of fairy lights, essentially strings of light bulbs. As the name suggests these conjure up the image of a cafe somewhere warm and lit, its terrace illuminated into the evening. These are lovely party lights, but equally they can be left out all year.

The brilliant thing about fairy lights is that it is very easy to track down solar powered ones, so you don't need to worry about connecting to the mains or installing an outdoor power-point. Lights are supplied with an adjustable solar panel that must be positioned so that they receive maximum daylight. The panel should be outdoors (rather than, say, behind a large window) and shadows shouldn't fall on it, particularly at the prime charging time, which tends to be between 10am and 2pm each day (depending on your climate). A solar-power panel is often adjustable so it can be angled for maximum sunlight at different times of the year. These lights can work all year round, although, obviously, they will receive a greater charge in the summer months. Those with smaller solar panels will struggle to power up in the short days of winter, so look for those with large panels, and they will keep on sparkling all through the winter.

ABOVE: Simple flames, used carefully, create lovelier effects than even the most expensive electric lighting system.

ELECTRIC-LIGHTING EFFECTS

You can of course create a number of effects with electric lighting, if that is to your taste – but try to keep it fairly subtle to avoid the 'corporate hotel' look. You might use spotlights to accent a particular shrub or feature, such as a large urn in a border.

Before going to the not-inconsiderable trouble and expense of having electric lighting installed to create effects like these, you might first want to experiment. Use a couple of high-powered torches, a camera (to record the results) and some amenable friends who don't mind standing in your shrubbery in the dark to offer their opinion.

Installing electric lighting in the garden is not a DIY job. Gardens are often wet places, and electricity and water don't mix. Employ a qualified electrician who will ensure that the correct cables are used and that every device is connected to a residual current device (RCD), which will automatically cut off the power in the event of an accident.

TYPES OF ELECTRIC-LIGHTING EFFECT

'**Grazing**' is when the light fitting is positioned close to the wall so that the beam of light 'grazes' its surface, picking out any slightly raised areas and throwing tiny recesses into deep shadow. This can create a very interesting effect, useful if you want to make a feature of a textured wall or other surface.

'**Moonlighting**' is an effect that involves positioning soft lights in the branches of trees to recreate the effect of moonlight and to cast soft, dappled shadows.

'**Shadowing**' and '**silhouetting**' are two sides of the same coin. 'Shadowing' involves lighting a particularly architectural plant from the front to cast a shadow on a wall behind. 'Silhouetting' involves lighting a similar plant from behind to create a strong silhouette when viewed from the front.

'**Uplighting**' is an effect that works best on well-shaped trees or groups of trees, or on statues, particularly where the statue is wider at the top than at its base.

A NOTE ABOUT WILDLIFE

Light pollution messes with migration patterns and confuses garden wildlife, so please keep all lighting minimal, with these animals in mind. Use the in-built timers on solar lights, and set timers on electric lights, so that your garden is dark when you are not using it and allow the night-time inhabitants of the garden to use the space in as natural a state as possible.

ABOVE: Electric lights can be used to make features look more dramatic; here they are used to silhouette gnarled vines.

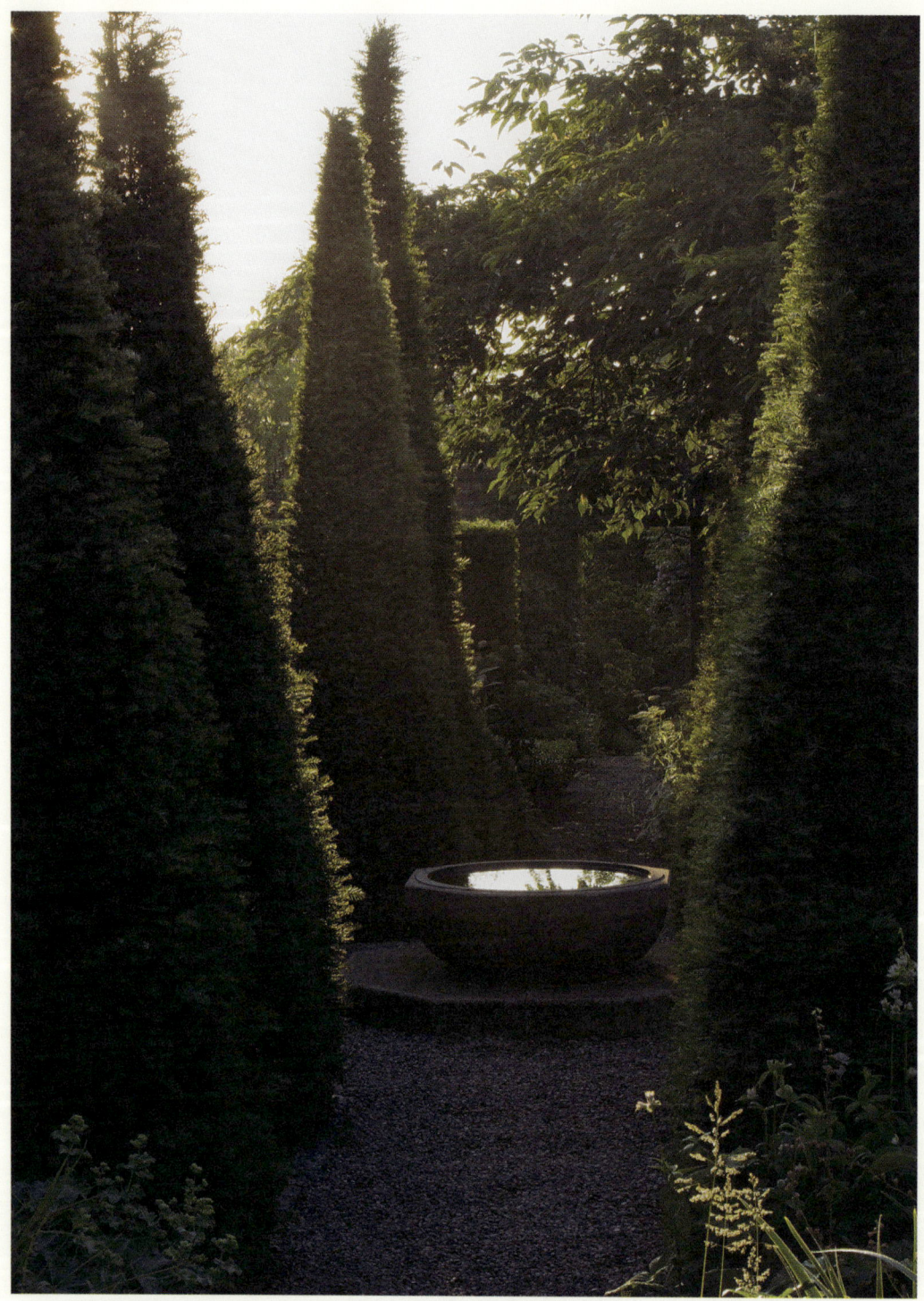

ABOVE: A small, still pool will reflect the moon and even – on particularly clear nights – the stars.

Using Water

A pond may not be the first thing you think of as a night-time feature, but it's wonderful for attracting wildlife. From the small and easily overlooked pond-skaters and beetles to the more glamorous dragonflies, newts and frogs, night-time wildlife-spotting is one of the most exciting aspects of the evening garden. If it is wildlife you're after, your pond shouldn't contain any fish, since these will prey on the other creatures in the water.

Your pond should have one shallow, beach-like edge where creatures can easily enter and exit the water. Fill your new pond with harvested rainwater or allow it to fill naturally with water directly from the sky. Any top ups should also be made with collected rainwater. Your pond will need planting with oxygenating plants such as *Elodea crispa* and *Deschampsia* (hair grass); deep-water aquatics such as waterlilies; and marginals such as *Lobelia fulgens*, calla and irises. These provide natural filtration and, with them growing well, the water will remain healthy and the pond will be able to sustain the maximum amount of wildlife.

Another night-time water feature to consider is a 'moon-gazing pond'. You can create one of these by positioning a small, still pool with a dark lining somewhere open so that the pool will reflect the moon unimpeded. Be warned, though, that if your moon-gazing pond doesn't contain any plants, the water will need changing frequently or it will quickly turn stagnant.

Moving water brings a garden to life whatever the time of day. In daylight hours, a water feature looks beautiful and provides lively, sparkling movement, but at night when the sense of sight is dulled and the other senses are more highly attuned, the sound of a water feature is particularly appealing. A small fountain trickling away in the darkness creates a wonderful atmosphere and helps, subtly, to mask any noises coming from outside the garden. A small wall fountain trickling into a basin of water makes a particularly lovely feature for a terrace or deck where you might sit during the evening. Consider building underwater lights into the basin that will light up the whole pond from below or, for a simpler but equally magical effect, place a handful of floating candles on the surface of the water instead.

Just as there is solar-powered lighting, there are solar-powered pumps and fountains that will reduce the cost and fuss of installation. These are generally designed for smaller water features, however. If you want a larger feature, such as a stream, you may have to use mains electricity to power your pump. Be extremely careful with any electricity and consult a professional for advice.

PART TWO

ENJOYING YOUR TWILIGHT GARDEN

MAKING THE MOST OF YOUR TWILIGHT GARDEN

It is very easy to get caught up in the 'doing' part of gardening and never get around to just *being* in it. The chores and tasks involved in garden upkeep are fairly enjoyable, after all — a little snipping and deadheading here and there, a quick mow of the lawn on a nice day — but for too many gardeners these become the whole experience of having a garden, rather than a means to an end. It is a great idea to think early on about exactly how you are going to relax in and enjoy the results of your labours – what are the occasions and activities that would suit you and your family at this stage of life? How can you draw yourself and other people out into your beautiful twilight garden for some leisure time?

This section is filled with ideas for how you might go about enjoying your twilight garden, from bonfire parties and moon-gazing to theatre nights, wildlife spotting and camp outs, with each idea requiring something slightly different to make it work.

ENTERTAINING IN THE GARDEN

You can have a party in any garden. A bit of music, a string of lights, a few chairs and some drinks, and you're away. However if you know you want to entertain in your garden (and you are at the garden planning stage), you might consider adding a few features that will make entertaining easier, and make you more likely to throw an impromptu outdoor gathering when there is a chance of good weather.

Consider creating a decent-sized patio or deck to act as a flat area that can be transformed easily into: a place for a table and chairs for meals, a dance floor, or even a stage.

A barbecue or a pizza oven and a surface for food preparation will make you much more likely to throw a spontaneous gathering. You can build your own barbecue cheaply with some loose bricks and a couple of grates.

A lawn comes in handy for larger parties, where you can put up a temporary gazebo and allow guests to spill out of the home. It is also perfect for picnics, especially for little ones.

Buy some garden furniture that you love: a table and chairs for eating around is a good place to start. Place this somewhere sheltered and maybe even covered if you're able to. Look for characterful second hand and vintage items to suit your style, though nothing overly fancy, as a life outdoors will take its toll – you can cover a chair with an oil cloth, tacked into place, to help keep rainwater off and prevent rotting, or extend its life by hammering on a large zinc sheet, which ages beautifully and creates a striking effect. Hardwood furniture will last well outdoors if oiled every year, but make sure it is certified by the Forest Stewardship Council, and so sustainably harvested. All garden furniture will last better if it can be put away or covered for the winter.

While a table and chairs for dining would generally be placed near to the house and close to the kitchen for bringing out food, have a think about other places, even in a small garden, where you might put a little seating area. A fire pit with seating around it tucked away at the end of the garden will make the space feel as if you're throwing a beach party or in the wilderness. You can buy iron fire pits that can be stored away when not in use, or you could consider making a dedicated area for a permanent fire pit. This should be a roughly circular area on the ground, lined with stones, bricks or pebbles, and seating can be as basic as some rounds of tree trunk. Situate fire pits away from the house, partly for safety reasons, but also so they are as far from the neighbours as possible. That way, you can sit up late and talk into the night without disturbing them. In a larger garden you might also put small seating areas around the garden, where small groups of people can gather separately.

You may want to create some privacy in your garden at dusk, as much for your neighbours' benefit as for your own in the case of night-time garden entertaining. Consider canopy sails that shield late-night fun from upper windows, and surround seating areas with dense plants that will muffle sound if you are outside late into the evening.

Lighting for parties should be of the flame- and fairy-lights variety. Fairy lights and bistro lights create just the right sort of atmosphere for entertaining. Flaming torches throw a very attractive light, but they need to be positioned with care for safety. The perfect place for flames is deep in borders, where they will look pretty but be well away from the revelers.

Finally select some good plants for party gardens, which will be minimal effort but provide maximum drama. Choose strongly structural, low-maintenance plants such as *cordyline australis* (see pp. 190–191), *choisya ternata* (see pp. 152–153) and *trachycarpus* (see pp. 192–193), and intersperse them with a few pale, scented flowers. *Trachelospermum* (see pp. 124–125) needs a support to climb up, but once you provide that, it looks after itself well.

Night-scented *hemerocallis* (see pp. 86–87) and evening primrose (see pp. 88–89) are good, low-maintenance perennial choices.

OVERLEAF: For spontaneous outdoor dinner parties you can bring indoor furniture outside. Just find cover for them if it begins to rain.

YOU WILL NEED:

A fire pit
A supply of dry wood
Lots of sparklers

REFRESHMENTS IDEAS

Part-baked baking potatoes, wrapped in tin foil and served with grated cheese
Marshmallows, for toasting whole
Hot chocolate
Mulled cider for grown-ups
Mulled apple juice for children

FOR SMORES

Biscuits e.g. Digestives or Crackers, graham if you can find them
Chocolate, milk or dark
Marshmallows
Tin foil
Tongs, for extracting

At Home Bonfire Night with Sparklers

On a chilly night, some people wrap up and head off for a big local fireworks display. There they might find masses of the noisiest, brightest and most beautiful fireworks, maybe even a musical accompaniment, some candy floss and even a few fairground rides. Fireworks events are bright, busy and noisy fun, but they aren't for everyone. Young children can find fireworks displays overwhelming, adults may want a less frantic time too, and if you have pets at home, you may want to stay close at hand to comfort them on this noisiest of nights.

Celebrations such as bonfire night in the UK, the Fourth of July in America, or New Year's Eve provide a perfect opportunity for a night-time gathering, which is a great excuse to have some fun in your garden. Invite a few friends and their families round to enjoy a fire pit and – possibly the best part of a bonfire night celebration – sparklers.

A small fire is all you need to keep people cosy and is a great way to have a fire in the garden without scorching the grass (too badly). Make sure the fire is situated away from overhanging branches, garden sheds and fences.

Part-cook some baked potatoes, wrap them in foil and place them in the embers. When you're ready to eat, fish these out carefully using barbecue tongs and eat them smothered with grated cheese.

When it's time for dessert, furnish everyone with sticks and marshmallows to melt over the fire. If it's cold, mulled cider will keep the adults warm; and mulled apple juice or hot chocolate will do the same for the children.

SMORES

Smores are an excellent dessert at your outdoor fire that everyone can get involved with. With this method, each person can make their own: take a piece of tin foil and place a biscuit on it, then a square of chocolate and a marshmallow, and finally top with another biscuit. Wrap tin foil around the whole creation and place it in the embers of the fire. Leave for at least ten minutes then remove with tongs. The marshmallow and chocolate should be melted and delicious. These are particularly good when dipped into mugs of hot chocolate or cocoa.

Star- or Moon-gazing Party

If you have your own telescope, the night-time garden becomes a place you are drawn to again and again. Even a simple and inexpensive bird-spotter's telescope can turn your garden into an opportunity to make a connection with the skies above. A star- or moon-gazing party can never guarantee results; and beware you may have to cancel at the last minute if clouds decide to drift across your part of the planet. However the uncertainty makes parties all the more special and memorable for you and your guests when things do work out.

To help your gazing-gathering go well, you need one of two things: a good moon or a celestial event. Of course, if you live in the country away from the light pollution which mars the city skies at night, then it's worth simply setting up your telescope on a clear night, inviting your friends round and seeing what you can see. Don't forget your star map.

In the city, though, options are more limited. You can see the moon and you can spot shooting stars if you time your party to coincide with a meteor shower. If you are moon-gazing, you really want the moon to be about half full, or just over, before you look at it through a telescope. When the moon is full, it's a bit glaring and too bright to look at, but when it's half-full, the light of the sun is falling across it, and this creates shadows, picking out the craters and giving a real sense of the detail of the moon. Even through a small telescope, you get a wonderful sense of the heft and solidity of Earth's natural satellite.

If you are stargazing in the summer, you won't have much trouble staying warm: you might need a jumper or two, and that's it. But in the winter, everyone needs to wrap up well. You don't want to light a fire to keep warm by and have its smoke cutting down visibility. Instead, go for hot-water bottles, blankets, rum-spiked hot chocolate (for the adults) and soup. That should do the trick while your guests gaze at the stars in wonderment.

SOME TIPS:

- Turn off garden lights and place yourself away from any direct source of light.
- Lie in sun loungers or on blankets on the ground, so that you get the full view of the sky above.
- Your eyes will take about 15 minutes to fully adjust to the dark – this is when you will start to see the full range of stars viewable from your location.
- During the party, it is important not to look at your phone, as this will set your eyes back.
- It can be a really good idea to use a star finding app on your phone. These will generally have night vision modes which will not interfere with your eyes.

ABOVE: A star- or moon-gazing event is an opportunity to appreciate the beauty of nature from wherever you are in the world.

YOU WILL NEED:

A telescope
A star map
Chairs or alternate seating
Hot-water bottles
Warm clothes
Blankets

REFRESHMENTS IDEAS
Soup e.g. tomato or pumpkin
Hot chocolate
Rum or whisky for hot toddies

THINGS TO LOOK OUT FOR WHEN STAR- OR MOON-GAZING

Get familiar with the cycles of the moon and try to catch it when it is at its first or third quarter. These times are when the light of the sun grazes across the surface, and you can pick out lots of detail with even a basic telescope or binoculars. Also, look out for news of astronomical events: lunar eclipses and occultations, and planets at 'opposition', which means they are at their closest to earth, and their brightest.

Meteor showers come around at the same time each year (see below) as they occur when the earth ploughs through the trails of dust left by certain comets in its annual pilgrimage around the sun. As the dust hits our atmosphere it burns up, creating meteors. These meteor showers are well worth looking for even under city night-sky conditions but be warned: treat meteor spotting in the same way as you might treat fishing. You may well catch a couple, but it is anything but guaranteed. Make this evening activity a beautiful occasion anyway, spending time out in the night-time garden with a flask and a friend, and keep your fingers crossed.

YOUR STAR GAZING CALENDAR – A METEOR SHOWER GUIDE

The Quadrantids are one of the earliest meteor showers of the year, spanning the end of December and the beginning of January, with the peak around 3rd January. The Quadrantids is also one of the most reliable meteor showers of the year.

The Lyrids run from mid- to late April with a peak around 23rd of the month. Look out for occasional 'Lyrid fireballs' which are bright enough to cast shadows and leave a dust trail for several minutes.

The Eta Aquariids run from the end of April to the end of May with a peak around 6th May. They are caused by Earth passing through the dust trail of Halley's comet.

The Perseids can be seen from mid-July to the end of August, peaking around 12th August. A prolific meteor shower, its meteors often have particularly long trails.

The Leonids occur in November and peak around the 17th. It has plenty of particularly fast-moving meteors.

The Geminid can be seen through December, peaking around the 14th. This shower produces an abundance of slow-moving meteors, which can make them easier to spot than others.

YOU WILL NEED:

A tent
Sleeping bags
Camping mattresses
Torches
Rugs
Cushions
Fairy lights

REFRESHMENT IDEAS
Sandwiches or hotdogs
Sauces e.g. ketchup, mustard
Soft drinks for the teens
A bottle of fizz for adults
A midnight feast of savoury snacks and sweets

Camping in the Garden

A garden at night can provide the first taste of independence, or a little adventure close to home. Camping in the garden sounds silly, but it is the perfect way to shake life up, to experience your own backyard from a different perspective, and to make a mini-holiday out of an ordinary day.

This is a particularly good activity for pre-teens and young teenagers: too young to go camping on their own but wanting to do something exciting. On a warm summer evening, have them invite a few friends over and let them camp in your garden. They'll experience the space and fun of a real camping trip but with parents and the safety of the house just a few steps away should anyone get scared.

Camping in the garden is not just for kids though. Gather a couple of your own friends or your partner, create a cosy hideaway, and light a campfire and fairy lights to make a memorable evening.

After setting up your tent, make the interior cosy with fairy lights and plenty of mattresses, rugs and cushions. You can use a few rugs on the grass near the fire, to keep everyone dry when they're sitting out. Have a few torches handy for when night falls. The beauty of camping in the garden is that you don't have to cook out there if you don't fancy it. Keep things simple – food you can eat with your hands, like sausages in buns with ketchup, and a big salad. Settle down around the fire and chat, tell stories and play music until you're tired enough to crawl off into your sleeping bags.

ACTIVITIES FOR A BACK GARDEN CAMP OUT

Anything you would play when camping is fair game for a back garden camp out, but you might want to pick games that you can do in a small space, (unless you have a football pitch sized garden yourself). Here are some suggestions for you to enjoy.

GAMES FOR YOUR CAMPOUT

Balloon off the ground: Blow up a balloon and toss it up into the air between you. Every camper does their best to prevent it from hitting the ground.

Ring toss: Set up cones or pins and aim to throw your ring to land on top of them. If it's too easy, throw in some harder levels: stand on one leg, with both eyes closed, or even turning your back and throwing the rings over your shoulder.

Charades: Good, old-fashioned fun. The person who is chosen selects a film, show, song or book, and then must act it out using no words. This game gets noisy but it is lots of fun.

Dominos and cards games: Gather everyone around inside the tent for a game of Dominoes, Blackjack, Cheat or Gin Rummy.

Scavenger hunt: Make a list of the items participants have to find and give each person a container to put them in. The winner is the first to tick all items off. Some examples are: a blue flower, a twig, a plastic dinosaur, a fallen leaf etc.

ABOVE: Camping in the garden creates everlasting memories, and gives you an adventure without ever leaving the house.

YOU WILL NEED:

Blankets, cushions, wooden benches or hay-bales for seating

Fairy lights, bistro lights, lanterns, candles or torches

Ivy, flowers, draped fabrics

A gazebo and umbrellas (in case of rain)

Theatrical material e.g. play or poems (home-made or borrowed)

Costumes e.g. cloaks, tunics, flower crowns and masks

Props (relevant to whichever performance you choose)

Music player e.g. an outdoor speaker or instruments

Hot spiced cider and food for a banquet

Theatre Night in the Garden

In the warm summer months, make use of the extra space a garden affords by putting on a performance. This could be done on any scale: from a simple poetry reading, where everyone reads a poem of their choice or of their own, up to a full-blown Shakespearean performance complete with costumes and lighting. *A Midsummer Night's Dream* – or readings from it – would be a perfect choice for a midsummer party.

Choose an area for your 'stage', ideally with a good backdrop – a wall or a bank of shrubs for instance. Look for a spot with trees or shrubs, that you can hang cloth from to make a makeshift theatre curtain for extra drama. Drape the wall with ivy and garlands of flowers. Light the stage area with fairy lights and bistro lights, and place lanterns and candles all around the garden.

Make a rank of seats facing the stage. You can have a jumble of chairs (borrowed from neighbours or friends), blankets and cushions on the ground or even some haybales for a rustic effect. Whichever seating you choose, provide lots of extra blankets and cushions so that your guests are comfortable as the night chills.

Ask your guests to dress up in a theme – and perhaps to bring their own chair if you don't have enough seating of your own. Depending on the form of the evening, you could also ask them to prepare a speech or a sonnet of their choosing.

This event would be a wonderful school holiday project for a group of friends or family with time spare during the long summer days. It could also make for a fun way to bring a group of friends of any age together to have a beautiful evening.

Follow the play with a banquet, laid out in the garden, and with hot spiced cider to warm everyone up.

Summer Barbecue

The ultimate occasion for enjoying and showing off your night garden is a summer barbecue. At this time of year, the weather is mild, the night-scented blooms are all doing their best work, and if you have delved into our planting guides you should have plenty of pale, summer flowers to impress your friends with as night falls. Good company, a few cold drinks, and a stunning setting will also make up for what might be mediocre food that is a bit burned around the edges and a bit raw in the middle. It's lucky that being outdoors makes you hungry.

FOR YOUR BARBECUE:

Site your barbecue somewhere safe where people can't knock it over if it's the flimsy kind, and where you won't set fire to any overhanging vegetation or to a shed or the garden fencing. The trick to a successful barbecue is to start it good and early. This gives enough time for the flames to lick away at the grill, then gradually subside, leaving just an ashy white covering to the coals. That's the time to start cooking.

Put the grill in its highest position above the coals so the food cooks slowly through to the middle. Prepare for the chance of grilling disaster by having plenty of salads on hand and some tasty fresh rolls.

Most barbecues start in the afternoon and drift on into the evening, so lighting them can be incidental. A few candles in jars here and there, scattered among your plants, will provide enough of a glow to prevent people stumbling into your flowerbeds, as the bucket of beer gets depleted.

TOP TIP:

Bunting turns even the most average garden into an instant party location. You can buy bunting, or make your own by cutting out triangles of fabric with pinking shears (which saves hemming) and sewing them to a length of ribbon. When finished string the bunting between fence tops and trees.

YOU WILL NEED

A barbecue and tools
Charcoal or fuel
Tables and seating
Napkins and plates
Candles in jars
Bunting

REFRESHMENTS IDEAS

Corn on the cob
Chicken thighs or wings
Vegetarian skewers
Sausage and hotdog buns
Burgers (meat and veggie options, if required)
Sides, e.g. potato salad, coleslaw
Beer, chilled in a bucket of water

ABOVE: Nothing unites friends and family like home-cooked food and joyous company.

My Classic Barbecue Chicken

SERVES 4

For the Marinade:
120 g/4¼ oz ketchup
60 ml/2 fl oz apple cider vinegar
50 g/1¾ oz brown sugar
30 ml/1 fl oz Worcestershire sauce
15 g/½ oz Dijon mustard
2 tsp smoked paprika
1 tsp garlic powder
1 tsp onion powder
cayenne pepper, sprinkle
salt and black pepper, to taste

For Cooking:
4 bone-in, skin-on chicken thighs
   (or same quantity of breast
   pieces or 8 drumsticks or wings)
15 ml/1 tbsp vegetable oil,
   for grilling
fresh parsley or spring onions,
   for garnish (optional)

In a bowl, whisk together the marinade ingredients, reserving 120 ml/½ cup of this mixture for basting later.

Place the chicken in a ziplock bag or a dish and coat with the basting marinade. Cover and refrigerate for at least 1 hour (or overnight for the best flavour).

Preheat the barbecue grill to medium heat and lightly oil the grill grates to prevent sticking. Place the chicken skin-side down and grill for 5-7 minutes, until the skin gets crispy and browned. Flip the chicken and cook for another 5-7 minutes on the other side.

Reduce the heat to low (or move the chicken to a cooler part of the grill) and cook for another 15-20 minutes, basting with the reserved BBQ sauce every few minutes for flavour and to keep the meat moist.

Using a temperature probe inserted into the centre of the meat, measure the internal temperature. Once this reaches 75 °C/167 °F, remove the chicken from the grill and let it rest for 5 minutes.

Garnish with fresh parsley or chopped spring onions. If you like serve with coleslaw, grilled corn on the cob, potato salad, or a fresh green salad. The marinade recipe can also be used to make a BBQ sauce on the side.

Wildlife in the Night-time Garden

It's more than a little exciting to find yourself sharing your evening peace and quiet with the snuffling of a hedgehog. In fact, there are lots of animals and insects that mainly come out at night, and you will make your garden a more interesting place to be at night if you learn how to encourage them in and cater for them.

HEDGEHOGS

Hedgehogs were once common in urban and suburban areas, but their numbers have declined dramatically, to the point where they are classified as 'vulnerable to extinction'. Only if you are very lucky will you hear one snuffling around in your undergrowth as evening falls. Creating a garden that contains plenty of food to their liking, and a variety of good nesting spots, will encourage any hedgehogs that come your way. Hedgehogs can travel over large areas in search of food, and they are surprisingly good climbers.

You can buy a specially made hedgehog home, which will provide a temporary nest for a few days in summer (hedgehogs tend to move around quite a lot when the weather is good) or a hibernation den in winter. You can make your own equally well in a quiet corner of the garden, using a couple of old bricks topped with a roofing tile and stuffed with leaves, twigs and straw. Alternatively, leave piles of twigs and foliage in the garden for the hedgehogs to make their own nests.

Any garden that is not too tidily managed is likely to prove attractive to hedgehogs. Hedgehogs eat slugs, snails, caterpillars and earthworms, so the best thing you can do to encourage them is to manage your garden organically. That way, you'll have plenty of food for the hedgehogs to devour. Avoid using slug pellets, since hedgehogs may be poisoned by eating slugs that have eaten the pellets. If you want to encourage hedgehogs with food, put some tinned pet food, raw or cooked meat, muesli or chopped peanuts out in the evening. If any food is left uneaten, bring it back indoors first thing in the morning. Don't put out milk and bread, as these can give hedgehogs stomach upsets.

MOTHS

Moths might be seen as the poor relative of the colourful butterflies that flitter around our gardens during the day, but they are beauties in themselves: subtler, far less showy and – admittedly – hairier, but if you can look at them up-close you will see that moths have stunning markings. Attracting moths is mainly a matter of good wildlife gardening: leave an area of long grass to flower and plant native trees and hedges which their caterpillars can feed on.

You can also plant night blooming flowers for nectar, which will attract and feed them on their night visits. Some varieties that are particularly good sources of nectar for moths include tobacco plants (see pp. 90–91), evening primrose (see pp. 88–89), honeysuckle (see pp. 94–95) and Dame's rocket (see pp. 84–85). Perhaps one of the reasons we fail to appreciate the beauty of moths is that, since they choose to come out after dark, we rarely see them. (See p. 74 for how to set up a moth lure.)

BATS

Swooping in at nightfall, bats are an incredibly exciting addition to night-time wildlife-spotting. Many bats are now endangered due to a loss of suitable places for roosting and a lack of available food – a situation that has partly been caused by intensive farming practices. By managing your garden organically, there is still a chance that you will get the occasional bat visitor. Bats feed on insects, so they like gardens that are teeming with prey. And if you have planted your garden full of night-blooming plants to attract night-flying insects, bats may well be lured in too.

As well as planting the night-blooming and night-scented flowers listed in detail in the second part of this book, try planting native wildflowers and simple cottage-garden perennials. Both do a better job of attracting plenty of insects to your garden, than highly-bred bedding plants and double-flowered varieties.

THE TWILIGHT GARDENER

Surprising though it may seem, another bat-attracting feature is a log pile, as these are great at providing a home for the insects that bats feed on.

Constructing a log pile is as easy as it sounds: you just need to gather a few logs and stack them up. The key then is to leave these logs to rot down; the more rotted they become, the more useful they are to insects. Choose a quiet corner of the garden where the logs are unlikely to be disturbed and, if possible, site the pile in shade where it won't get heated up and dried out by the sun.

If you have a suitably quiet, undisturbed spot, you might also consider putting up bat boxes. These look like bird boxes except they're entered from below, so there's a hole where there would otherwise be a floor. Bat boxes need to be on the north side of a tree or building (depending on your location) so the sun doesn't shine directly on them during the day, which is when the bats use them. It can take a long time for bats to find bat boxes, so be patient and don't take yours down just because you don't get any residents for a couple of years.

GLOW-WORMS

Imagine sitting outside your back door and watching the soft, green glow of glow-worms providing tiny pinpoints of pale green light around your garden. These garden visitors make the perfect finishing touch for any garden at dusk. Glow-worms aren't worms at all but a type of beetle. In this species, it is the females that glow to attract a mate. They are extremely rare, and in truth you are fairly unlikely to be able to lure them onto your patch, but by having a go, you will also be creating a garden that other forms of wildlife will love even if you don't attract glow-worms themselves.

Glow-worms prefer some grass left long, although they also like to have an open area to display themselves. To ensure that they will be seen, female glow-worms only start to glow when it's really dark, meaning they won't hang around where there is artificial light. They also need pesticide-free gardens and some damper areas where there will be lots of small snails to feed on. Hedgerows and ponds seem to attract glow-worms, too. Look out for glow-worms on dark, moonless nights between late spring and early autumn. If you spot any in your garden, consider yourself extremely lucky, and try to keep the conditions to their liking.

Ways to Spot Night Wildlife

You can of course just spend time in your garden in the evening and hope for a chance wildlife sighting, but here are a few other ways to check whether you are being visited.

MAKE A MOTH LURE

The simplest moth lure is made by hanging a white sheet on the washing line or elsewhere in the garden, any time in the summer months, and leaving a bright torch shining on it. Within minutes it should be covered in moths. You can try to identify the moths by sight (or you can buy an identification guide to help you) as they flit about, but you might find identification easier if you catch them in glass jars. Take great care not to damage the moths if you do this and release them as soon as you can. Children love being involved in this activity, and it's a great way to lure them out into the garden of an evening. A sheet on a washing machine is the budget-friendly way of doing this but can be a little hit and miss too. A UV 'catch and release' moth trap is expensive but a more certain way of viewing the moths in your garden. You leave these traps out all night to view and release your catches the next day.

MAKE A FOOTPRINT TUNNEL

This is a lovely way of seeing what animals have been visiting your garden at night. You will need: a piece of cardboard, masking tape, white paper, a dish of cat or dog food, some vegetable oil, and some food grade activated charcoal powder, or readymade footprint tracking ink. Fold your piece of cardboard lengthways twice so that it can make a triangular tunnel. Open it and place the food dish at the centre, a few strips of tape on either side to make an 'ink pad', and then the white paper. Tape down the paper. Rub some vegetable oil onto the masking tape and sprinkle on the carbon powder, then tape up the top two edges of the cardboard to form the tunnel. Place it alongside a fence, in some thick growth, or anywhere you think animals might travel through your garden at night. Check your tunnel in the morning and compare it with an animal track guide. To reuse, you can simply wash and refill the food dish and replace the ink and paper at any time.

SET UP A WILDLIFE CAMERA

Although it is wonderful to spot or hear wildlife when you are sitting quietly in the garden in the evening, your very presence reduces the chance that creatures will feel comfortable enough to be there. Wildlife cameras and trail cameras can be set up to take pictures and videos in your absence and can reveal a world of nocturnal wildlife activity. Look for a camera with night vision and remote viewing capabilities, which means you will be able to monitor activity as it is happening or play back footage without having to retrieve the camera. Attach the apparatus to a sturdy branch or post in a spot where you suspect animals pass by, or need to a feeding station, and prepare to enjoy the show.

PART THREE

PLANTS AND PLANTING

STAR PLANTS

The plants that will make your evening garden look special are those that are light-coloured or pure white. These will glow in the gloom of early evening or reflect back any glint of moonlight. The star plants in your evening garden should be these – lots of pale beauties to catch the eye after everything else has faded into the background.

But the evening garden is about all the senses; perhaps even more important than the sense of sight is the sense of smell. As darkness kicks in, all the plants in this section start to produce scent. A few are fresh with a citrus kick, but most are heavy and spicy, rich and intoxicating. These seem, appropriately enough, to be the scents of the night. Plant as many of these flowers as you can get your hands on. Each will add its own individual character to the evening breeze and will make your garden a place that you are constantly drawn to at night.

Angel's Trumpet

Brugmansia suaveolens

Situation:	Full sun
Hardiness:	Frost-tender (USDA zone 9)
Soil type:	Any good potting compost
Height:	3 m/9 ft 9 in
Spread:	1.5 m/5 ft
Propagation:	From cuttings in summer in a heated propagator, or sow seed in spring
Planting:	Plant out after danger of frost has passed
Flowering period:	Throughout summer and autumn
Toxicity:	All parts potentially poisonous

The scent of brugmansia (often commonly known as datura although not, strictly speaking, the same plant) is utterly intoxicating. It is said that if you fall asleep beneath one, you will have nightmares, and it's easy to understand why. The scent hangs in the air, heavy and penetrating. Brugmansia's common name is angel's trumpet, thanks to the huge, trumpet-shaped flowers that hang down dramatically from the stems. A well-grown plant covered in flowers is an extremely impressive sight. The flowers come in shades of red, orange, coral, pink, orange and white, with the white ones said to have the strongest scent.

However, all the flowers are so strongly scented that you needn't worry too much about the gradations between them. They are all completely over the top.

These vigorous plants will put on a good metre (3 ft) or even two (6 ft) of growth in a year in the right conditions, but they're not at all hardy so must be protected from frost. You will need a greenhouse that is kept at a minimum temperature of 7°C/44°F all winter. If you're not able to heat a greenhouse to this temperature, you could try bringing the plant indoors over winter. Ideally, you should place it in one of the cooler spots in the house, such as a minimally heated spare room. Only take it outdoors again once you are certain that all frosts have passed and the evening temperature is noticeably mild.

Plant brugmansia in a large pot in spring (remembering that you will need to be able to move the pot indoors again in the autumn) and use a good multi-purpose compost. Start watering and feeding as it comes into growth. To get the vigorous growth that will lead to the best flowering, give these plants huge amounts of water and feed them almost whenever you think of it; they will gobble it all up.

As they grow, they send up forking stems. Don't prune these back as it is only after these stems are produced that the plants will flower.

Red spider mite can be a problem in dry weather. These tiny pests are barely visible so they are easy to miss. They suck sap from the leaves and slowly weaken the plant, discolouring the leaves and leaving a fine web across them. The mites thrive in dry conditions and hate humidity, so give the whole plant a regular watering (leaves and all) or mist with the fine nozzle on the hosepipe each evening to discourage them.

Be warned that all parts of the plant are poisonous.

Citrus

Citrus

Situation:	Full sun
Hardiness:	Tender (USDA zone 11)
Soil type:	Well-drained
Height:	2 m/6 ft 6 in
Spread:	1 m/3 ft 3 in
Propagation:	From cuttings in summer
Planting:	Keep indoors until frosts have passed
Flowering period:	Mainly spring and summer, but can flower all year round
Fruiting period:	Mainly in winter, but can fruit at other times
Toxicity:	Non-toxic

Citrus trees make beautiful, glossy little plants for a conservatory or patio. Their leaves are deep green and highly polished, and the white, waxy flowers, as well as the leaves, are sweetly citrus-scented. This is a plant that smells as strongly in the day as it does at night, but it adds a fresh, sharp note to other night-time scents.

Several of the citruses make particularly good pot plants. Lemons, limes and calamondins are the easiest to overwinter successfully, so these are the best choices for beginners. They're not hardy, though, so before any hint of a frost – ideally in early autumn – you will need to put them in a frost-free greenhouse (heated to at least 4°C/40°F) and move them back outdoors for the summer. If you don't have a heated greenhouse, place your plant near a brightly lit window, ideally away from any radiators or direct sources of heat.

It is a good idea to pot citrus trees on once a year into a slightly larger pot, top-dressing with fresh compost at the same time. One problem with this is that the plants get bigger and need larger and heavier pots, yet still need to be moved each year. A small trolley can be the solution: just make sure you place the tree onto the trolley while you can still lift it.

You can buy specialist citrus composts, but they are not really necessary. Instead, just add plenty of horticultural grit to the compost to keep it free-draining.

Citrus trees like a slightly acidic soil: if you want to avoid using a peat-based ericaceous compost, sprinkle sulphur chips on the surface of a normal compost. One of the problems that often besets citrus plants is yellowing of the leaves. This is caused either by the soil being too alkaline or by a lack of feed. Use a specialist citrus fertiliser every few weeks during the growing season. As well as keeping the plant well fed, it will help maintain the soil at the correct pH level.

Dame's Rocket

Hesperis matronalis

Situation:	Sun or partial shade
Hardiness:	Hardy (USDA zones 3–9)
Soil type:	Humus-rich but well drained
Height:	90 cm/36 in
Spread:	45 cm/18 in
Propagation:	Sow seeds in early spring
Planting:	Plant out in late spring
Flowering period:	Late spring to late summer
Toxicity:	Non-toxic

Dame's Rocket or sweet rocket lives a double life. During the day, it is the perfect, sweet, pretty cottage-garden plant. It rubs along beautifully with other cottage-garden perennials and attracts bees and insects – especially butterflies – from all around. Come evening, its strong, spicy scent kicks in and spreads throughout the garden. You will quickly find that moths love it just as much as butterflies do. As well as the name sweet rocket, it has a number of other common names, many of which allude to its smell or its place in the evening garden. These names include dame's violet, damask violet, eveweed and mother-of-the-evening.

Dame's rocket was first grown in England in the sixteenth century, which is perhaps why it looks so completely at home in a cottage garden setting. Plant it with alliums, hardy geraniums and roses to pull off the complete cottage-garden look with ease.

The species *Hesperis matronalis* is a pretty biennial or short-lived perennial that bears loose panicles of pale pink or purple flowers on tall stems throughout summer, from late spring well into late summer. *H. m.* var. *albiflora* is the white-flowered version and smells just as good, with the added bonus that the flowers show up better at night. Both last well as cut flowers, so if the summer weather isn't good and you are not managing to sit out and enjoy the evening scents, you can at least cut yourself a few sprigs to enjoys indoors.

Being a short-lived perennial, your plants will start to fade away after a few years and the flowers will gradually become fewer and fewer. Luckily, this plant self-seeds with abandon. All you need to do is thin out the seedlings to allow a few plants to grow full-size each year, and you will have them in perpetuity. If you want to move self-sown seedlings to a new part of the garden, do so whenever they are large enough to handle easily. If you find they're becoming a pest and you want to stop them self-seeding, try to remember to cut off the spent flower spikes before they go to seed.

Should you want to start new plants from seed, you should sow a thin row in spring on a spare patch of soil or in a nursery bed that has been well worked and raked to form a fine tilth. When the seeds germinate, thin them out to around 30 cm/12 in apart. Transplant them to their final planting places in autumn and the plants will start flowering in the summer of the following year. New plants will need watering in dry weather while they are getting established.

In their native habitat, these plants are woodland dwellers and can tolerate partial shade or full sun. The soil should be moist but well drained and should echo the soil found in a woodland setting, which means that it should contain plenty of organic matter. Leaf mould makes the perfect addition to the soil and will help keep the plants happy and their roots moist.

Daylily

Hemerocallis

Situation:	Sun or partial shade
Hardiness:	Hardy (USDA zones 3–9)
Soil type:	Moist, humus-rich
Height:	1 m/3 ft 3 in
Spread:	75 cm/30 in
Propagation:	From divisions in spring or autumn
Planting:	Plant out in spring or autumn
Flowering period:	Early to midsummer
Toxicity:	Very toxic to cats

A plant with the common name of day lily might not seem an obvious choice for an evening garden, but the name refers to the fact that each of the day lily's flowers opens for just 24 hours or less. Most open in the day and fade towards night, but the flowers of *Hemerocallis citrina* open in mid-afternoon, are in full bloom by evening and continue through the night. It produces a lemony scent, with hints of honeysuckle. The flowers fade early the next day, but throughout midsummer there is always a succession of buds waiting on the prolific flower stalks.

The flowers are fine and delicate, with thin, pale yellow petals. They are arranged in a star-like fashion, slightly recurved at the tips. The pale yellow shows up well in low light.

Day lilies form generous clumps of long, thin, shiny, strap-like leaves. They are herbaceous perennials, so they die down over the winter. Spring and autumn are when you should lift and propagate them. Use your garden fork to loosen the soil around the plant, then lift the whole clump. Plunge two forks back to back into the centre of the clump to prise it into two pieces. You can either replant the pieces immediately or pot the divisions in containers of fresh compost. Do this every few years whether you want to propagate or not, as clumps will flower less as they get larger and more congested.

Day lilies like a rich, fairly moist soil. They grow well in partial shade, but produce more flowers in full sun. Remove the individual spent flowers to encourage more flowers to form as well as to keep the plant looking tidy. When all the buds on a flower stalk have opened and faded, cut the stalk right back to its base. When the leaves have died back you can pull them off. Mulch all around the plant with a thick layer of compost or well-rotted farmyard manure in spring. If it is to form the maximum number of flower buds, the day lily's roots need to be moist throughout spring, so start watering when growth first starts and continue throughout spring if the weather is dry.

Evening Primrose

Oenothera biennis

Situation:	Sun
Hardiness:	Hardy (USDA zone 4)
Soil type:	Well drained
Height:	1 m/3 ft 3 in
Spread:	60 cm/24 in
Propagation:	Sow seeds direct or in pots in early summer
Planting:	Plant out in autumn
Flowering period:	Early summer to early autumn
Toxicity:	Non-toxic

The yellow flowers of the evening primrose open late in the day, as evening falls, and they do so surprisingly swiftly. They're loved by both day-flying insects, such as bees and butterflies, and by night flyers such as moths. In the evening it's their sweet perfume that mainly attracts pollinators, and it is this that makes it worth growing in the twilight garden. The evening primrose produces tall flower spikes, each bearing many cup-shaped flowers along its length. The flowers open pale yellow and age to a darker yellow with a hint of green. This colour combination makes them really luminous in low evening light, although the younger flowers glow the most brightly.

Evening primroses are at their best when planted in well-drained sandy soil, since heavy clay soils can lead to rotting during the winter. If you have to plant them in heavy soil, mix plenty of grit into the planting hole as well as into the area around it, to allow water to drain away. They like plenty of nourishment, too, so dig lots of compost or well-rotted manure into the soil.

Being a biennial – which means it will grow leaves in its first year, flower in its second year, then die – evening primroses should be propagated from seed in early summer. Sow them any earlier than this, and the plant may get large enough to attempt to flower, but it will be a weak and puny attempt and will stop the plant from growing big and beefy for a great show the following year. Sowing in early or midsummer should be perfect.

The seed is very fine indeed. It can be sown direct where it is to grow, then thinned out later, or sown thinly onto the surface of soil in pots, then thinned out. In autumn, the young plants should be put in their final planting positions and kept well-watered while they get established. They will flower from midsummer the following year.

Cut back the flower spikes as they go over. Once the final flower has finished, you can either leave it in place and allow seeds to form, in which case it is very likely to self seed, or you can pull the whole plant out and compost it.

Despite being short-lived, since evening primrose self-seeds so readily, you should always have a succession of younger plants coming along. Once it has decided it likes your garden, you are unlikely to need to do much to encourage it. In fact, it can become a bit of a weed, albeit a very lovely one. The best way to prevent it becoming too much of a problem is to snip off the flower spikes before they have a chance to go to seed.

Flowering Tobacco

Nicotiana sylvestris

Situation:	Full sun or partial shade
Hardiness:	Half-hardy annual (USDA zone 8; annual elsewhere)
Soil type:	Moist, woodland-type soil
Height:	1.5 m/5 ft
Spread:	50 cm/20 in
Propagation:	Sow seeds in early spring
Planting:	Plant out once frosts have passed spring
Flowering period:	Throughout summer
Toxicity:	Toxic to dogs and cats

Nicotiana is possibly the most famous night-scented plant. With its huge, 1.5 m/5 ft spires of dangling white flowers, it makes a massive impact in the night garden and would be an impressive plant even without its scent.

One of the most remarkable things about *Nicotiana sylvestris* is that it's an annual. This means that it has to put on massive amounts of growth, produce bucketfuls of flowers and, if you let it, seed – and all in a few short months.

To give it the best chance, you need to start the small seeds off good and early in the spring. Sow them on the surface of a fine, well-sieved seed compost and water in. Ideally, place the seed trays or pots in a heated propagator to ensure good germination. Grow on in a greenhouse and, when the weather gets warmer, slowly harden the plants off by putting them outdoors during the day and bringing them back indoors at night. You should eventually plant them out in the garden around late spring.

At first, the plants will form a rosette of paddle-like leaves, then the huge flower spikes will start to emerge. These will be topped with green buds that open to reveal pure white, star-shaped, drooping flowers with improbably long, thin necks. These prove much too delicate for the job, so the flowers dangle gracefully, unable to hold their heads up. The effect is like a particularly classy, pure white firework.

Children love this plant: it towers over them, jungle-like, with its huge leaves and explosions of flowers. Thanks to its sticky, hairy leaves, it also gets plastered in tiny, dead flies. This goes down well with kids who are attracted to all things gruesome; less well with children of a more sensitive disposition. During the day, it smells of nothing, so children usually miss out on the big show. By dusk, the scent starts to kick in, sweet and strong and, as night deepens, it only gets stronger. Moths love these flowers – they use their long proboscises to probe deep down the dangling throats and access the nectar held at the base of the flowers.

Plant nicotiana in full sun in soil that has been well prepared with lots of garden compost or well-rotted farmyard manure. Choose a fairly sheltered spot, out of strong winds, as the tall stems can be blown over or end up leaning if the wind is strong. You can stake any plants that are having trouble staying upright by pushing a bamboo cane firmly into the soil and then tying the flower stalk loosely onto it with twine. Cut off faded flower heads to encourage new flushes of flowers, but leave some flowers on if you want them to self-seed.

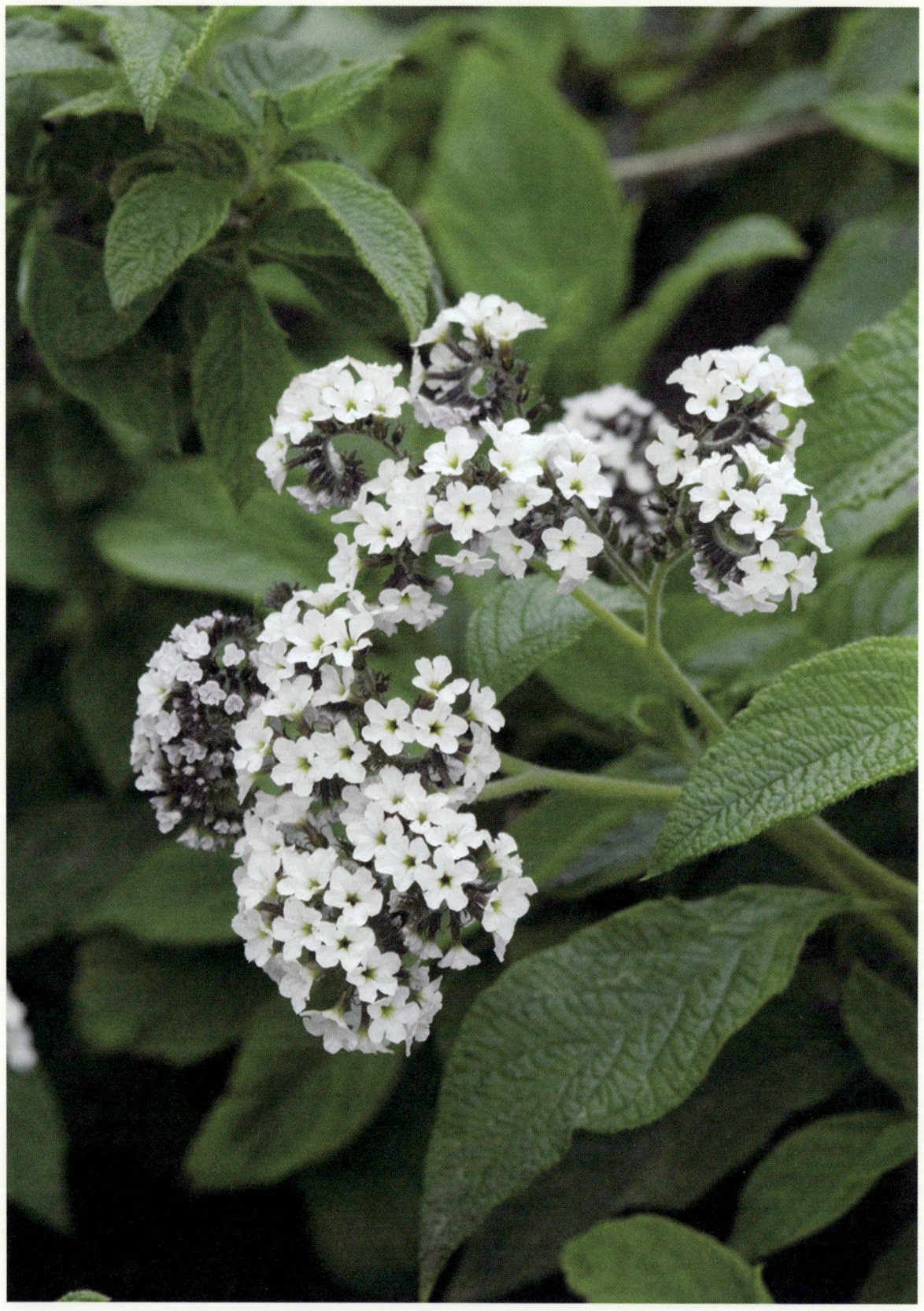

Heliotrope

Heliotropium arborescens, Nautilus White

Situation:	Full sun
Hardiness:	Half-hardy; grow as an annual (USDA zone 10)
Soil type:	Moist, well drained
Height:	30 cm/12 in
Spread:	20 cm/8 in
Propagation:	Sow seed in early spring
Planting:	Plant out after danger of frosts has passed
Flowering period:	Summer
Toxicity:	Toxic if ingested

Heliotrope is commonly known as cherry-pie because of its intense, sugary-sweet, vanilla-essence-like smell. The small purple flowers usually grow in a dome shape, but there are white-flowered forms, too, and these are even more strongly scented. The plant is strong-smelling both during the daytime and at night.

Heliotropes are small, compact plants that look good in a summer bedding container or in a window box. They need a spot in full sun in order to flower at their best. They are actually short-lived, half-hardy shrubs, but it is tricky keeping them going from year to year, so they are most often grown as annuals. You may find them on sale as bedding plants in garden centres in spring. The purple-flowered, compact 'Marine' is the most commonly grown cultivar. 'White Lady' is one of the white-flowered cultivars.

Sow the seed thinly in early spring in a tray of levelled and firmed seed compost. Cover the seed with compost, then water in or sink the tray into a bath of water so it soaks water up. Let it drain, then place the tray in a heated propagator in good light. Prick the seedlings out into individual pots when they are large enough to handle. Plant them out only after you are fairly sure that the last frosts have finished. If you have a greenhouse, you can plant them into your outdoor mixed containers before the frosts are over and keep them there so they grow on and mingle with the other plants. If colder weather is forecast after you have put the containers outside, you can always swathe the entire pot in horticultural fleece to protect it. Water the plant freely when in growth and feed every couple of weeks with a general fertiliser.

A temperature lower than −2°C/28°F is likely to kill heliotropes, so if you want to overwinter them, you will have to keep them in a frost-free greenhouse. You can take cuttings in summer, but you'll have to overwinter these in a frost-free greenhouse. Keep any overwintering plants just moist: don't overwater.

Honeysuckle

Lonicera japonica 'Halliana'

Situation:	Partial shade
Hardiness:	Hardy (USDA zones 4–9)
Soil type:	Moist, humus-rich
Height:	10 m/32 ft 9 in
Spread:	3 m/9 ft 9 in
Propagation:	From cuttings in summer
Planting:	Plant out in autumn or spring
Flowering period:	Summer
Toxicity:	Highly toxic to humans, cats and dogs

If you're the generous sort and want to give your neighbours as magical an experience of night-time gardening as you are planning for yourself, trying planting honeysuckle. It is the ultimate evening garden plant, producing great wafts of honey-like scent that permeate the summer evening air. If it is allowed to really romp away and clamber up a large tree or over a sturdy pergola, honeysuckle will perfume the air of the entire neighbourhood. Planting one is a truly benevolent act.

The flowers are made up of clusters of long, tubular flowers that bear the scent. As a rough rule of thumb, the less showy the flowers, the greater the scent. This means that the pale yellow flowers of *Lonicera japonica* 'Halliana' release one of the strongest scents, yet the vivid orange and red *L. j.* 'Dropmore Scarlet' is almost entirely unscented. Unfortunately, you have to choose between looks and smell. That's not to say that the scented honeysuckles are ugly, but they are not fine and delicate, so they look their best in a woodland or cottage-garden situation.

Honeysuckles are, in fact, originally woodland plants. This makes them quite handy in the garden since they can tolerate a fair bit of shade. If you want something that will cover a north- or east-facing wall and still produce flowers, honeysuckle is a good bet. Honeysuckle climbs by means of lax, twining stems rather than with suckers, so it needs quite a bit of help to get it moving skywards. This means you will need to provide a support system. A trellis (but not one with small squares, as the honeysuckle's long stems can't weave their way through) offers reasonable support, but not once the honeysuckle really gets going. Parallel wires stretched across a wall approximately 30 cm/12 in apart work much better. Choose good, thick wire for the job: once the honeysuckle gets big and heavy, it will quickly pull thinner-gauge wire out of place. During the growing season, you should regularly tie the stems to the support, or at least twine them around it if they are not doing so themselves. Since honeysuckle is a woodland plant, it will appreciate a moist, humus-rich root run.

Use plenty of leaf mould or compost in the planting hole and mulch with more of the same once a year.

Honeysuckle often suffers from powdery mildew – a fungus that manifests as a white powdery coating on the leaves. It occurs when the roots become dry. Unfortunately this happens fairly often with climbers that are planted near walls and fences, as these cast a 'rain shadow' that prevents rain from reaching the soil. So plant your honeysuckle as far away from the wall as possible and lean the plant into it. Remember to water it in dry weather.

Japanese Wisteria

Wisteria floribunda

Situation:	Full sun or partial shade
Hardiness:	Hardy (USDA zone 5)
Soil type:	Moist but well drained
Height:	9 m/29 ft 6 in
Spread:	9 m/29 ft 6 in
Propagation:	By layering in autumn
Planting:	Plant out in spring
Flowering period:	Early summer
Toxicity:	All parts are toxic

Wisteria is always impressive. It romps away, twining its stems over its supports and, come early summer, it produces masses of racemes of 30 cm/12 in-long, pendent flowers. The effect is almost like a waterfall. As the stems mature, they very quickly take on a gnarled, characterful appearance that makes the plant look good even when it is not in leaf or flower.

Most wisterias, though not all, are scented, however *Wisteria floribunda* and its cultivars have a stronger scent at night and so they make a wonderful addition to the night garden.

W. floribunda is also slightly less rampant than some other wisterias, but it's still a huge plant and needs a large support. You can grow it through a tree, which is how it grows in the wild, but to do this you will need to plant it away from the tree and leaning in towards it. To begin with, you may have to help it along with a bamboo cane or similar so that it can reach the tree. Once it does, you can tie it in to the tree, after which it should look after itself.

Wisteria looks wonderful trained against a house wall, but for this you will have to fix a series of parallel wires to the wall to act as support. (You can use a trellis, but it would have to be huge.) It is also the perfect plant for covering a well-built pergola; here the flowers will hang down completely unimpeded and will look their best.

Wisterias have a reputation for being slow to flower, so to avoid a long wait you need to take care when buying. Plants grown from seedlings can take up to fifteen years to flower for the first time, but if you buy a plant that has been grafted onto a rootstock, it should flower in its first or second year. Ask when you buy, or look for the knobbly graft low down on the stem.

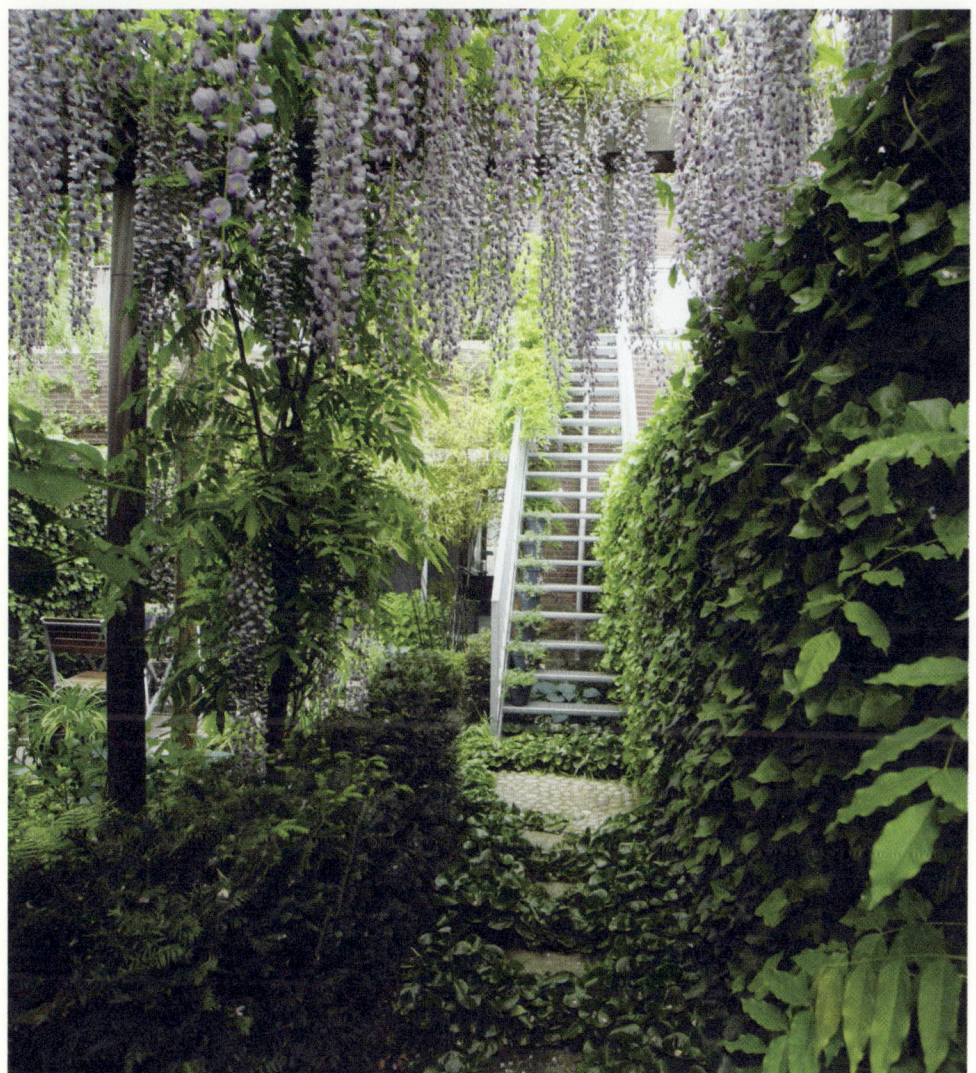

Soil next to walls can be very dry since the rain doesn't reach it, so if you are planting a wisteria against a wall, plant it as far away as possible and lean it in towards the wall. Improve the soil before planting with garden compost or well-rotted farmyard manure. Plant in spring or autumn, then water well. If you are planting in spring, keep the wisteria well watered throughout summer. As it grows, train the shoots along the support.

Pruning is important to keep the plant within bounds and to encourage flowering. Ideally, pruning should be done twice a year, in late summer and in winter. In late summer, cut back any side shoots that aren't needed to extend the basic framework, leaving about six leaves on each shoot. In winter cut these back for a second time, leaving three buds.

Wisteria produces green seed pods in summer. Make sure children don't get hold of these, or any other parts of the plant, since they can cause extreme discomfort if eaten.

Jasmine

Jasminum officinale

Situation:	Full sun or partial shade
Hardiness:	Frost-hardy to −5°C/23°F in a sheltered spot (USDA zone 7)
Soil type:	Humus-rich, slightly moist
Height:	12 m/ 39 ft 4in
Spread:	10 m/32 ft 9 in
Propagation:	From cuttings in summer
Planting:	Plant out in spring
Flowering period:	Summer
Toxicity:	Non-toxic to humans, mildly toxic to animals

Jasmine's long, fine, deep green stems twine up a support. In summer it is smothered in small, pure white, star-shaped flowers, which show up well against the dark background created by the fine leaves. You might even call the plant delicate if it weren't quite such a romper. Jasmine is a truly vigorous plant once it gets going. It will cover a pergola in no time and can even be used to clothe a small garden building or to help you disguise an ugly fence or wall.

The flowers emit a strong, sweet fragrance that is particularly strong in warm, sheltered spots. In fact, you will have to choose the sunniest and most sheltered spot in your garden for this plant, as jasmine is only hardy to around −5°C/23°F, so it will struggle in harsher winters. Tucked away in a warm, sunny corner, the plant will fare better.

The plant is semi-evergreen or deciduous, so it will keep some of its leaves during milder winters. Don't expect it to provide a great deal in the way of evergreen winter structure, however; jasmine has a tendency to look pretty ropey in winter, although it quickly leaps back to life come spring.

Jasmine needs a sturdy support to climb up. A set of parallel wires fixed to a wall or a chunky trellis will be perfect. You may need to help it start climbing up a pergola, so tie the shoots in loosely to begin with. Then, once the plant has wrapped itself around the pergola supports sufficiently, you can remove the ties.

The main problem with jasmine is keeping it under control. It grows extremely quickly and will outgrow all but the very largest of supports if not pruned occasionally. The best time to prune is just after flowering. Bear in mind that flowers are borne on stems that are at least a year old. In other words, if you cut the plant back completely, you will have a whole year to wait until the stems are mature enough to bear flowers.

When pruning, aim to remove up to one-third of the oldest flowered stems each year. If the plant has become completely overgrown and this seems too fiddly, you can chop it back hard. If you do this, do it in spring and give it plenty of mulch, feed, water and care afterwards.

Jasmine likes a soil that contains plenty of moisture, but doesn't like to sit in water over winter. Before planting, improve the soil with plenty of organic matter such as leaf mould to keep the soil moist but free-draining. Mulch with leaf mould or garden compost once a year.

Lily

Lilium regale 'Album'

Situation:	Full sun
Hardiness:	Hardy (USDA zone 8)
Soil type:	Rich and fertile but well drained
Height:	1.5 m/5 ft
Spread:	30 cm/12 in
Propagation:	Lift bulbs in autumn and separate offsets to grow on
Planting:	Plant out in autumn or spring
Flowering period:	Midsummer
Toxicity:	Toxic, highly to cats

Lilies provide one of the must-have scents of the summer – rich and sweet, and at its strongest and most delicious on a warm evening. Their tall stems reach up above other perennials and the large, trumpet-shaped flowers gaze down elegantly over the garden. A good-sized clump of these pure white lilies is a majestic sight and will fill the evening garden with scent.

Lilium regale has white flowers, but the backs of the petals are pink. *L. r.* 'Album' is exactly the same shape, but with petals that are entirely white and with a particularly strong fragrance. Asiatic and Oriental lilies really need to be planted into containers, but *L. regale* and its cultivars are surprisingly tough and can be planted out in the garden where they'll slowly clump up. Plant them among clumps of perennials.

Buy the lilies as bulbs in spring or autumn. It can be hard to get hold of lilies in autumn, but if you can find them and get them planted at that time of year, the roots get a chance to develop during the winter and you will get a better display in the first year. On the other hand, there is generally a better choice of bulbs in spring.

Choose a planting spot where the bulbs and roots will get some shade but where the growth and flowers will be in full sun. A spot among ground-cover perennials such as hardy geraniums is perfect. The soil needs to be rich and moist, but water must drain away easily as the bulbs won't put up with sitting in water over the winter. Adding a mix of compost, leaf mould and grit to the planting hole will ensure you get the balance right. If you are planting in a container, put plenty of crocks in the base to ensure the drainage hole doesn't get blocked with compost, then use a mixture of good, peat-free multi-purpose compost and grit.

Whether in pots or in the soil, you should plant the bulbs as early in the year as you can manage and you should plant them deeply, with about 12 cm/5 in of soil above them. After flowering, feed with a high-potash fertiliser such as tomato fertiliser or comfrey liquid. This will help build them up for the following year. If you are growing your lilies in pots, it is important to keep them evenly watered while they are in leaf, as drought can affect flowering.

The main problem that afflicts lilies is the red lily beetle. This beautiful scarlet fiend lays its eggs on the undersides of the foliage. As the grubs hatch and grow, they cover themselves in a brown sticky substance and start eating away at the leaves. An unnoticed infestation can strip the foliage in a few days. Inspect the undersides of leaves regularly for rows of red eggs and for the grubs, and squash them on sight. Kill the adults, too, when you spot them.

Marvel-of-Peru

Mirabilis jalapa

Situation:	Full sun
Hardiness:	Frost-hardy (USDA zone 9)
Soil type:	Well drained
Spread:	60 cm/24 in
Height:	60 cm/24 in
Propagation:	Sow seed in spring or take divisions in spring
Planting:	Plant out in early summer
Flowering period:	Throughout summer
Toxicity:	Roots and seeds mildly toxic

Mirabilis jalapa, which goes by the impressive common name of marvel-of-Peru, is one of the few night-scented plants with colourful flowers. But if you think this plant will bring a splash of daytime colour to a garden designed for evening, you'd be wrong. Its other common name is four o'clock plant: the flowers stay tightly closed until late afternoon, then the cool of the evening triggers them to open. The flowers are vibrant deep pink, paler pink, yellow and white, all on the same plant, and they can change colour as they age – yellow to pink, white to purple. They're also strongly fragrant, with a sweet, orange-blossom-like scent. Come morning, the individual flowers wither and die, but throughout summer there is always a succession of flowers waiting to bloom the following evening.

These are perennial plants that are just about frost-hardy, meaning that they will survive a fall in temperature to −5°C/23°F. The first light frost cuts the top growth down. The tuber that is left in the ground may survive the winter, particularly in mild areas and if the ground has been covered in a thick, dry mulch, such as bark chippings, after the plant has died back. Alternatively, you can lift the tuber after the first frosts and overwinter it as you might a dahlia tuber. Brush off the dirt, nestle it in some sawdust or vermiculite and store it in a dark, frost-free place until early spring. Then bring it out, plant it up and water it, keeping it in a frost-free place until all danger of frost has passed.

Mirabilis will grow quickly and flower freely in its first year when grown from seed, and that is how it is usually treated. The seeds are large and germinate easily. Sow them in early spring in a frost-free place, pricking them out into individual pots when they are large enough to handle and planting them out after the last frosts. Choose a spot that receives full sun, is sheltered and has a reasonably well drained soil. Alternatively, you can plant them into containers, which will allow you to bring them up close to seating areas where the scent can be appreciated. In autumn it is easy to save the big, black seeds for growing the following year. Store these in a cool, dry place.

When the plants are young, the new growth is particularly susceptible to aphids. Check young plants frequently and squash any aphids you see. If you get a bad infestation, it can really slow growth, particularly when the plant is young and just getting going. Frequent misting of the plant with a very mild detergent solution (a small drop of washing-up liquid to a mister of water) can help keep aphids under control.

Moonflower

Ipomoea alba

Situation:	Full sun or partial shade
Hardiness:	Tender; grow as an annual (USDA zone 10)
Soil type:	Fertile, well drained
Height:	4 m/13 ft
Spread:	2 m/6 ft 6 in
Propagation:	Sow seed in spring
Planting:	Plant out in early summer
Flowering period:	Summer to autumn
Toxicity:	Seeds are toxic

The moonflower, *Ipomoea alba*, is a vigorous twining climber that clambers up supports. It has large, dark green leaves and produces huge, white, trumpet-shaped blooms. The flowers stay tight shut against the sunshine during the day, then open at night in a swift movement, taking only about a minute to unfurl. Once open, they emit a strong, sweet, moth-attracting fragrance.

Moonflower grows quickly to cover a support, but it isn't hardy so will only last one season. Despite growing as a perennial in warmer countries, in colder climates it is most often grown from seed each spring as an annual. The seed coat is hard, so the seed can be slow to germinate. To soften the coat, soak it in tepid water for a few hours before sowing. If the seed is particularly large and tough, nick it with a knife or rub it onto sandpaper to break through the seed coat before soaking it. Sow several seeds to a pot or scatter them across a seed tray filled with seed compost. Cover with compost and water in.

When the seeds have germinated, transplant them into individual pots of fresh compost. Keep them well watered in a warm, light spot. You can plant them out once all danger of frosts has passed, either direct into the soil or in a large container filled with peat-free multi-purpose compost. Wherever you put them – but especially if they are in the ground – you will need to take care to protect them from slugs. Keep the plant well watered throughout summer and feed every couple of weeks with a high-potash fertiliser such as tomato fertiliser or comfrey liquid. At the end of the season, the plant will be killed off by the cold weather.

Although this plant is an annual, it's a big one (you could use it to hide an ugly wall) and needs a strong support, such as a wooden trellis or system of wires, to clamber up. To begin with, you will have to tie the first growths loosely to the support to help the tendrils attach to it. They are unlikely to need any more help than that, but check from time to time and tie in more growths if necessary.

Night-blooming Jessamine

Cestrum nocturnum

Situation:	Full sun or partial shade
Hardiness:	Tender; grow as a house plant (USDA zone 11)
Soil type:	Moist but well-drained
Height:	1 m/3 ft 3 in
Spread:	1 m/3 ft 3 in
Propagation:	From cuttings in autumn
Planting:	Plant out after danger of frost has passed
Flowering period:	Summer
Toxicity:	Mildly toxic to humans and pets

This intensely, almost intoxicatingly, fragrant little plant needs to be grown as a house plant for most of the year, but it is worth the fuss. Commonly known as night-blooming jessamine, its unusual smell is quite unlike that of jasmine (the derivation of its common name) and more like a delicious spicy incense. It is widely planted in subtropical gardens, where it stays out all year long. Despite the plant's small stature, it has a very strong scent. It will waft across your garden, filling it with its tropical smell, while indoors it is so overwhelming that you will certainly want to move it outdoors for the summer.

Cestrum nocturnum is a small evergreen shrub with glossy, dark-green leaves. In summer it produces clusters of slender, tube-shaped whitish-green buds all along its stems, the ends of which open into little star-shaped, pure white flowers. Planted out in warmer climates, cestrum will grow to about 4 m/13 ft in height and spread. When you don't have the luxury of planting it in the soil, it is important to keep pruning it so that it's small enough to bring indoors as a house plant. The time to prune is just after the flowers have faded. Cut the stems back fairly hard, by about half, to stimulate new growth from lower down the plant and keep it bushy and compact.

Use a good peat-free multi-purpose compost and mix in plenty of grit to aid drainage. Water thoroughly throughout the summer and let the plant dry out almost completely before soaking it again. Feed once a week with a high-phosphate fertiliser such as tomato fertiliser or comfrey liquid. In winter keep the plant very dry and in a light, well ventilated spot. You can keep it in a greenhouse or conservatory, but don't let the temperature drop below 5°C/41°F. If you can't manage this, keep it indoors in one of the cooler spots in the house.

Cestrums often drop their leaves in winter but, as long as you don't overwater them, they should leap back into life come spring.

Keep these plants out of reach of children or pets: all parts are toxic.

Night-scented Phlox

Zaluzianskya ovata

Situation:	Full sun
Hardiness:	Frost-hardy (USDA zone 9)
Soil type:	Moist but well drained
Height:	25 cm/10 in
Spread:	30 cm/12 in
Propagation:	From cuttings in summer
Planting:	Plant out in spring
Flowering period:	Throughout summer
Toxicity:	Non-toxic

This low-growing, compact perennial from South Africa is a tiny, truly pretty plant that packs a huge punch scent-wise. It forms a dome of evergreen aromatic leaves and in midsummer is smothered in long, dark-red tubes topped with small deep-red buds. These open to reveal pale, pinkish-white inner petals, each one scalloped and gently cupped to reveal the strong contrast between the inner and the outer petals.

On summer mornings, the flowers start to open but, as the sun gets hot, they clamp shut again. It is only in the cool of the evening that they open fully and waft their spicy, sweet, complex honey-like aroma through the garden. It is very impressive for such a small plant and moths love it.

Zaluzianskya is half-hardy, which means it will tolerate a temperature of −5°C/23°F. In all but the mildest areas, you will have to grow it in a pot so it can be moved to a cool greenhouse or even a cold frame over winter. If you are planting it into the soil, it needs a rich, moist soil, but it must be well drained so the plant doesn't sit in water over winter. Mix in plenty of compost and grit when planting to try to achieve this tricky balance.

That's another reason why this plant works best in a pot: you can control the watering much more easily. It likes to be kept good and moist during the summer but fairly dry during winter, and that's hard to achieve when it is planted in the soil. Throughout summer, water frequently and feed once a week with a fertiliser that is high in flower promoting potash, such as a tomato fertiliser or comfrey liquid.

These are short-lived perennials so they will gradually run out of steam and need replacing. They can also turn woody quickly if allowed to dry out in summer. If they do this, it's an indication that they are nearing the end of their useful lives. They

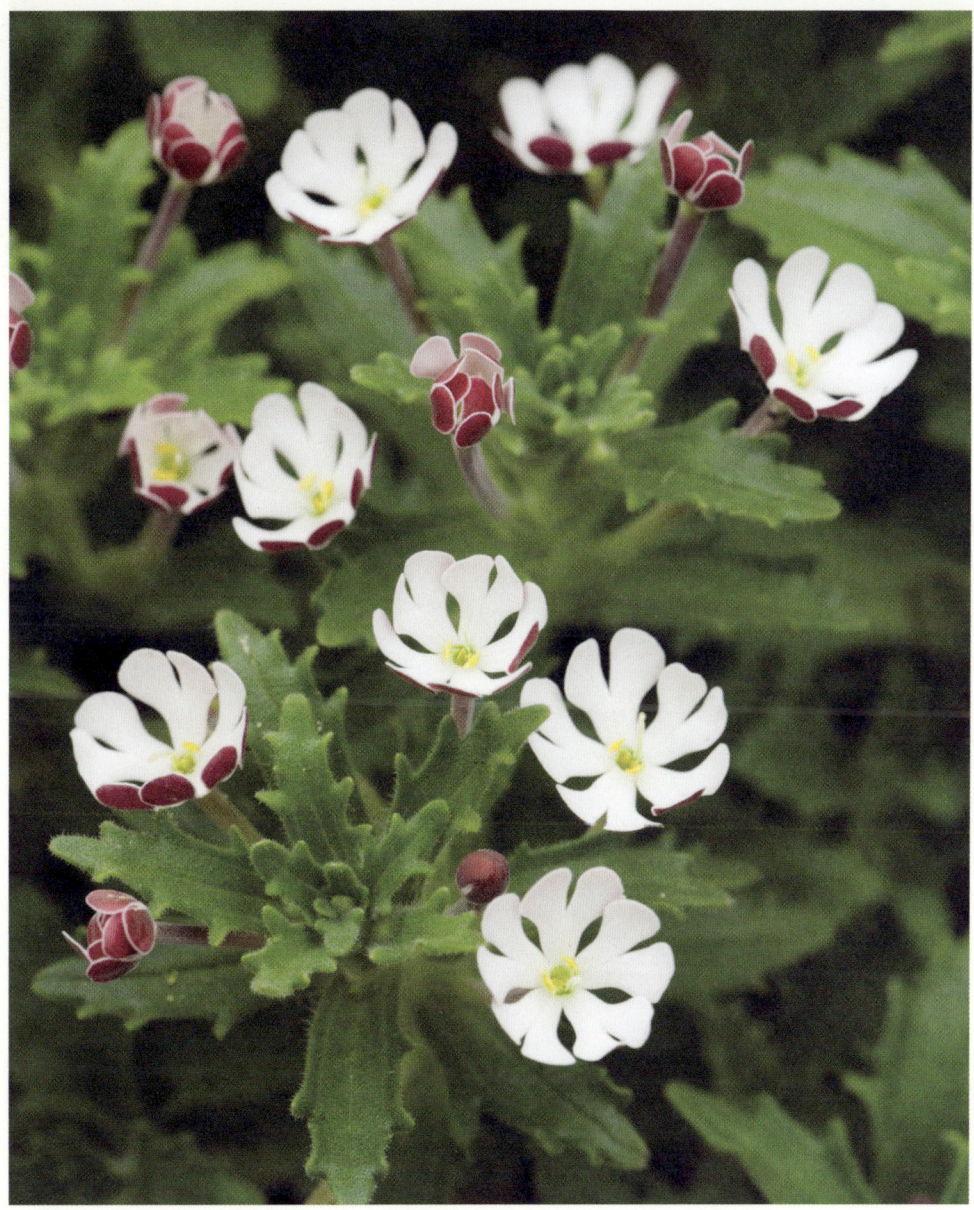

generally stay fairly compact so you don't often have to cut back or prune, but it's a good idea to take cuttings each summer to ensure you always have young plants coming along as replacements. Take cuttings from non-flowering shoots and push them into pots of compost-and-vermiculite mix or compost-and-grit mix. It is a good idea to cover the pots with a clear plastic bag to keep them humid, and keep them cool and shady while the plants are taking root. Pot them on individually once they have rooted. You will need to overwinter these small plants carefully and plant them into larger pots for the patio the following spring, moving them outdoors when all chance of frost has passed.

Night-scented Stock

Matthiola bicorni subsp. *bicornis*

Brompton Stock

Matthiola incana

Situation:	Partial shade
Hardiness:	Hardy (USDA zones 4–9)
Soil type:	Moist, humus-rich
Height:	10 m/32 ft 9 in
Spread:	3 m/9 ft 9 in
Propagation:	From cuttings in summer
Planting:	Plant out in autumn or spring
Flowering period:	Summer
Toxicity:	Highly toxic to humans, cats and dogs

The annual night-scented stock, *Matthiola bicornis*, isn't much to look at in the daytime. The pale greenish-grey stalks and leaves are fairly sparse and the plant can look a bit rangy. The flowers are even slightly shrivelled. But as night falls, the petals unfurl and you get small, pink or pale purple star-shaped flowers that pump out a spicy clove-and-vanilla scent that fills the garden. Because of their slightly wild appearance, these stocks look best combined with other plants in a cottage-garden border, rather than in a container where they would look a little sparse, particularly during the day.

As an annual, this stock should be sown in spring. You can sow it direct where it is to flower and thin it out later, but you will achieve better results if you sow into a seed tray or small pot and pot it on or thin it out later. The seedlings are very small and you may need to pot them on in small clumps, rather than trying to pot them on individually. Plant out as soon as the plants are large enough.

M. bicornis will self-seed fairly readily if it finds a spot to its liking, so if you want it to return, make a point of learning what the seedlings look like so you can avoid them when you're doing the weeding.

Matthiola incana is a short-lived perennial that is also sweetly scented. It produces short, stout flower spikes smothered in four-petalled flowers. There are many pretty cultivars that are useful as bedding plants for the evening garden. Some of these are double and so create a fuller, more voluptuous effect than the annual stock, although the scent isn't as impressive. They are available in a range of strong pinks and

ABOVE: Night scented stock provides one of the most lovely scents in the evening garden, and is very easily grown from seed, so you can fill your borders with it.

purples through to paler colours. Their stature and colour make them a great choice for a summer container in a twilight garden.

If you're lucky, you might find the perennial stock in the bedding section of your garden centre, among the bedding geraniums and lobelias. But you can't always rely on this, so if you are keen to feature this plant in your twilight garden, you would do best to grow it from seed, just as you would night-scented stock (see above). Make sure you grow the perennial stock in plenty of light so that the plants don't become leggy.

Both plants require a warm, sunny position to grow at their best, and they prefer to be sheltered from the wind, too.

Petunia

Petunia Tumbelina Series

Situation:	Full sun
Hardiness:	Half-hardy (USDA zone 10; annual elsewhere)
Soil type:	Moist, well drained
Height:	40 cm/15 in
Spread:	30 cm/12 in
Propagation:	Sow seed in spring or buy as young plants from the garden centre
Planting:	Plant out when all danger of frosts has passed
Flowering period:	Summer
Toxicity:	Non-toxic

Petunias aren't the most highly esteemed plants. Classier gardeners regard them as a bit common and brash – not quite the thing. That may be because they are so popular and are often used in bright, clashing colour mixtures. Come spring, they are on sale in every garden centre and in summer they seem to be in every hanging basket and bedding scheme.

In fact, petunias are extremely floriferous, hard-working plants. They're also night-scented (some smell in the daytime, too, but you have to get really close and have a good sniff). In the evening they emit a faint scent, but they really come into their own in the dead of night, when they produce wafts of sweet vanilla-like scent. They might be most appreciated by late-night revellers returning home in the small hours.

Petunias are a mainstay of any summer bedding display. They have a very attractive habit, with trailing stems that are absolutely smothered in trumpet-shaped or frilly double flowers all summer long. You can plant a hanging basket or container entirely with petunias or you can make the most of their trailing habit by using them to soften or even hide the edges and sides of a mixed container. Avoid the clashing-colour problem by choosing your petunias carefully. A container of pale petunias combined with the silvery foliage of the bedding plant 'Silver Dust' (*Jacobaea maritima*), for instance, is perfect for a twilight garden.

The Tumbelina and Wave series are among the more highly scented petunias. You may struggle to track these down at planting-out time, so you may prefer to grow them from seed. Sow in early to midspring. The seed is really tiny and hard to handle, so mix a small amount with a teaspoonful of silver sand, then sprinkle the mixture onto the surface of a seed tray filled with firmed, levelled and wetted compost. Don't cover with compost. Place in a heated propagator in a well-lit place. When the seeds

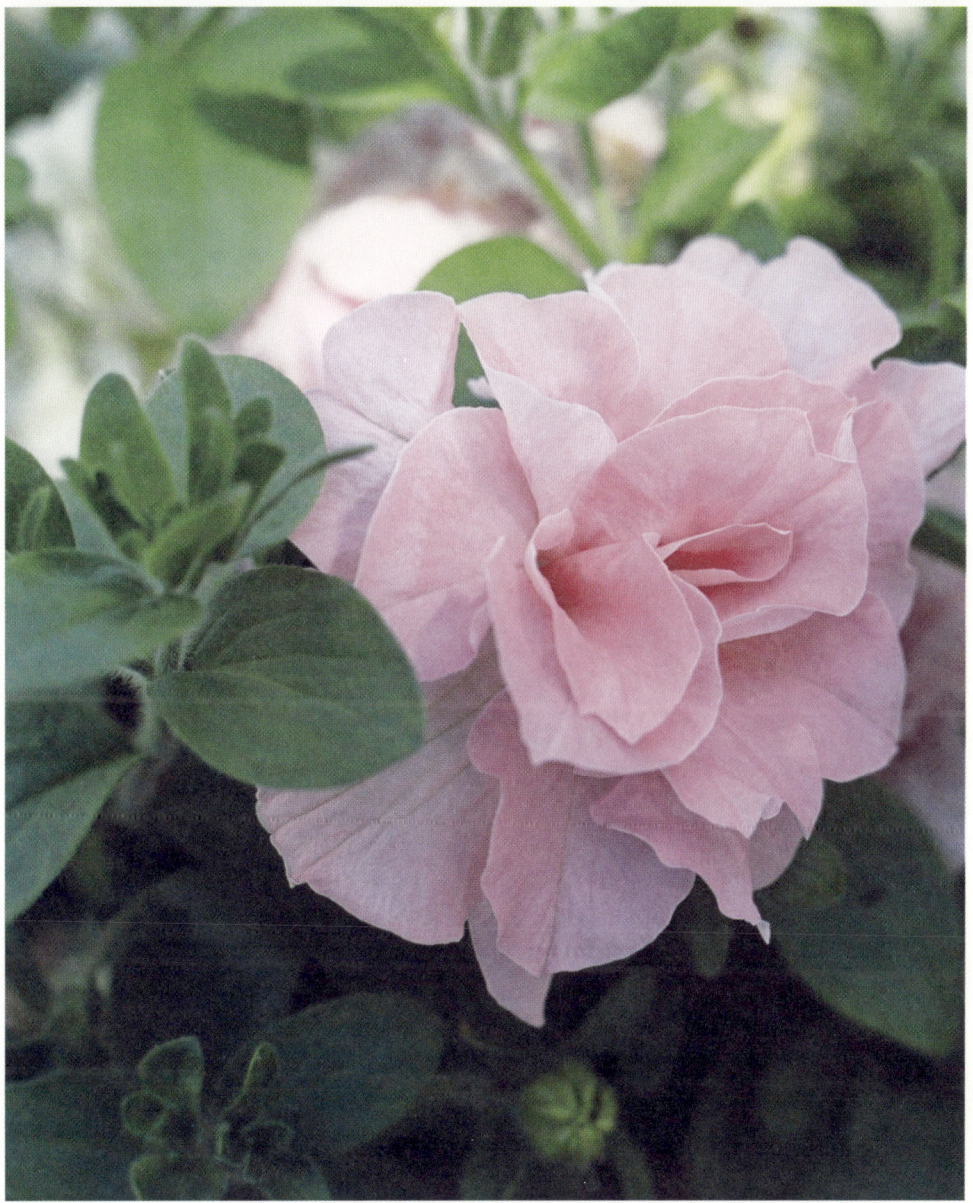

have germinated, pot them on in small clumps then, when these are large enough to handle, pot them on into separate modules.

When all danger of frost has passed, you can plant the modules – as well as any garden-centre plants – in your outdoor containers, but be ready to protect them with fleece if there are warnings of late frosts.

If you have a greenhouse, you can pot up your outdoor containers fairly early in the spring and grow them on in the greenhouse so they look full when you put them outside.

Pink 'Mrs Sinkins'

Dianthus 'Mrs Sinkins' (p)

Situation:	Full sun
Hardiness:	Hardy (USDA zone 8)
Soil type:	Chalky/alkaline, well drained
Height:	25 cm/10 in
Spread:	30 cm/12 in
Propagation:	From cuttings in summer
Planting:	Plant out in spring
Flowering period:	Early to midsummer
Toxicity:	Contact with the leaves can cause some skin irritation in children

Pinks such as dianthus 'Mrs Sinkins' produce a delicious clove scent during the day, but the fragrance is even stronger at night. This isn't a plant that pumps scent out across the garden in the same way that, for instance, lilies do, but it will add a spicy layer to the smell of your night garden. Many of these dianthus are pale in colour, too, so they will stand out in the darkness.

Dianthus have been a favourite with gardeners from around the seventeenth century. They form neat mounds of grey-green foliage that make attractive ground cover and are a beautiful foil for other flowers even when they aren't in flower themselves. They come in colours ranging from white and pink through to crimson, maroon and blackcurrant, and many are patterned. 'Mrs Sinkins' is an old variety that has been in cultivation since 1868. In early and midsummer, it produces pure white double flowers that are prettily fringed at the edges and give out a particularly strong, rich scent.

Dianthus thrive in well-drained chalky soils and may struggle in a clay soil. Before planting in a heavier soil, mix lots of grit in and around the planting hole and add ground limestone. You may also need to put limestone around the roots regularly to keep the plant happy. These plants are drought-tolerant and will fare well in dryer areas, but they won't tolerate sitting in water and the stems will quickly rot. Plant them in a slight mound of soil so they are lifted above any standing water.

Consider using dianthus to edge your borders: they have a lovely, low-growing habit and will spill out neatly over pathways. They can also be planted in gaps in paths or patios where, again, they will spill out over the paving. They look great in a Mediterranean border full of other silver-leaved plants, or in a gravel garden, but they're most at home in a cottage-garden border, planted towards the front.

If you don't have the right type of soil, it is best to plant dianthus in containers rather than battle to make your soil suitable. You can then keep them near so you can enjoy the scent, or even put the pots on a table for your evening enjoyment. They do well in containers because they are drought-tolerant and can put up with a little neglect, but they will do best if you remember to water them frequently while they are in active growth. If you have them in pots, feed them regularly over summer with a balanced fertiliser. In the autumn, do a small tidy-up, cutting back long, straggling stems to make a neat mound that will look good all through winter.

Queen of the Night

Epiphyllum oxypetalum

Situation:	Dappled shade
Hardiness:	Tender; grow as a house plant (USDA zone 11)
Soil type:	Epiphytic cactus compost
Height:	2 m/6 ft 6 in
Spread:	1 m/3 ft 3 in
Propagation:	From cuttings in spring
Planting:	Should not be planted out but can spend a spell out of doors during the warmest summer weather
Flowering period:	Late spring and summer
Toxicity:	Non-toxic

Epiphyllum oxypetalum is an epiphytic cactus, which means that, in the wild, it perches soil-less in the crooks of trees and similar spots. It has large, fleshy, rangy leaves and a quite crazy, untidy habit of growth, flinging stems and leaves out this way and that. You can try to contain it a little by wrapping a piece of garden twine around the stems to pull them together, but it really doesn't like to conform. It is also completely **tender** so can't be left outdoors all year round except in subtropical areas. This means you must grow it as a house plant in winter and can move it outside for summer. You can leave it indoors if you wish, but the scent can be quite overwhelming.

Epiphytic cacti have different needs from other cacti. Your average cactus wants a compost composed almost entirely of grit and to bake in full sun, whereas epiphytic cacti like a loose, low-nutrient compost with plenty of gaps in it – chunks of bark make a good addition. You can buy forest cactus compost or make your own from a mixture of sand, normal potting compost and part-composted bark chippings.

These cacti like dappled shade and will get burned in full sun. Once all chance of frost has passed, find them a spot outdoors, out of direct sun, for the summer. Water freely when in growth, particularly in hot weather. From early spring, apply a high-potash fertiliser such as tomato fertiliser or comfrey liquid to encourage flowering. Reduce the watering in winter, but don't let the plant dry out completely.

Cuttings take easily, particularly if struck in spring. Simply cut a leaf off and push it into a pot of compost mixed with sand or grit for drainage. Keep the pot somewhere warm and light but out of direct sunlight. A north- or east-facing windowsill is ideal. Keep the compost just moist. It has rooted when new shoots appear.

Soapwort

Saponaria officinalis

Situation:	Full sun or partial shade
Hardiness:	Hardy (USDA zone 4)
Soil type:	Well drained; tolerates poor soils
Height:	30 cm/12 in
Spread:	20 cm/8 in
Propagation:	From divisions in autumn
Planting:	Plant out in spring or autumn
Flowering period:	Summer into autumn
Toxicity:	Non-toxic

Common soapwort, sometimes also known as bouncing bett, is an easy-to-grow hardy perennial with pale pink flowers that release a sweet scent at night. Hailing as it does from meadows and rocky, mountainous areas, this is a useful plant that grows well in poor, gravelly soils. In fact, soapwort is best confined to such soils as there is a risk of it becoming invasive in gardens where the soil is too rich.

There are some more compact, less invasive cultivars, but soapwort is generally a big grower so is best planted where it can spread to its heart's content and alongside strong, vigorous neighbours, such as Japanese anemones. They are definitely worth growing, though. They look good in borders with other cottage-garden perennials, are hugely floriferous, and will create an incredible bank of night fragrance with no trouble at all. Plant soapwort in spring or autumn in well-drained soil in full sun or partial shade. If you are planting in the spring, keep well watered, particularly during dry spells, until the plants are established. If you are planting in autumn, you may need to water a little until the plants die down for winter, but after that they will probably take care of themselves.

Soapwort has a fairly floppy growth habit, so it is a good idea to have some support in place around the plants before the new shoots emerge in spring. This is better than supporting them once they have grown large: perennials supported later on always look rather trussed-up and awkward. You can use plant-support rings or bamboo canes or simply use any offcuts from shrubby pruning that are left over from your winter trimming.

After flowering, deadhead the plants, cutting back into the stems a little. This encourages growth from the base, keeps the plant from flopping too much, and sometimes leads to a second flush of blooms.

Perennials like this one die down in winter, leaving dead stems behind. You can leave these on the plant or cut them back to tidy the plant up for winter, but it is now generally regarded as good practice to leave the dead stems on so insects can overwinter on them. You can, however, have a little snip every now and then if they get too messy. Cut all stems down to the ground in spring.

It is simple to propagate soapwort from divisions in autumn.

Star Jasmine

Trachelospermum jasminoides

Situation:	Full sun or partial shade
Hardiness:	Frost-hardy to −5°C/23°F in a sheltered spot (USDA zone 7)
Soil type:	Well drained but moist in summer
Height:	9 m/29 ft 6 in
Spread:	9 m/29 ft 6 in
Propagation:	From cuttings in a heated propagator in summer, or by layering in summer
Planting:	Plant out in spring
Flowering period:	Mid- to late summer
Toxicity:	Non-toxic

The star jasmine, *Trachelospermum jasminoides*, is a gentler, calmer and, if truth be told, classier, version of the true jasmine. This is an aristocratic plant that has everything going for it – glossy, dark, evergreen leaves that turn slightly reddish in winter, and deliciously jasmine-scented flowers in summer. The flowers are small, white and star-shaped with a slight twist at the centre.

The problem with trachelospermum is the opposite to that of jasmine. Whereas jasmine races away and is almost impossible to contain, trachelospermum is slow to get going. It creeps along, taking several years to really get into its stride. But this is also one of its charms. You don't have to keep cutting it back, for a start. It will stay fairly neatly in a relatively small area, and pruning can be of the delicate snipping variety, rather than the panicked hacking type. But don't be too hasty with the pruning: you will get the best show of flowers if you can encourage the plant to grow upwards and then to cascade down. The flow of sap is restricted on stems that hang downwards, which discourages soft green growth and encourages harder, flowering wood to form.

In theory, trachelospermum is self-clinging, so you shouldn't need to provide support, but in reality its clinging powers are fairly weak. It definitely needs quite a lot of help to get started when first planted: tie the stems in loosely to a support. And if you want your more mature plants to cascade forwards without pulling themselves off the wall, you will certainly need to provide the support of a few wires or a sturdy trellis.

Trachelospermum's slow, steady nature also means that the growth has a pleasingly woody, mature character. The whole plant looks solid and well built – as if it's here to stay. It can be a little shy to flower, so the trick is to plant it in your sunniest spot.

In fact, it is only frost-hardy, so it doesn't appreciate temperatures lower than −5°C/23°F. It really needs the warmth of a sunny south- or west-facing wall to grow well and won't thrive if it is subjected to cold winds.

To propagate, you can either take cuttings or layer the plant. Take 5–7½ cm/2–3 in cuttings in late summer. Remove the lower leaves, insert a few cuttings around the edge of a pot of gritty compost, then root them in a heated propagator. Layering involves taking a low-lying stem and pinning it to the ground with a tent peg or similar. Making a small nick on the underside of the stem where it touches the ground can help it to form roots. Once it has rooted, sever the rooted section from the plant and pot it on.

Tuberose

Polianthes tuberosa

Situation:	Full sun
Hardiness:	Frost-tender (USDA zone 9)
Soil type:	Well drained but moist
Height:	90 cm/36 in
Spread:	15 cm/6 in
Propagation:	From offsets in autumn
Planting:	Plant out in summer, they will need to be brought in and kept frost-free over winter
Flowering period:	Summer
Toxicity:	Mildly toxic

The tuberose is possibly the most strongly scented of all the night plants. It has an intense, heavy, decadent fragrance that is produced by tall spikes of thick, waxy, star-shaped, double, pure-white flowers. The plant would be worth growing for its exotic beauty alone, even if it didn't smell delicious. 'The Pearl' has an even stronger fragrance than the species; in fact, it's almost a bit much.

One of the tuberose's common names is mistress of the night. It will make you work hard for its scent, though: it's a bit of a diva and certainly isn't a plant you can throw in the ground and forget about. Hailing as it does from Mexico, it's not surprising that the tuberose likes a bit of heat. It can be left to grow in a pot all summer if you like, then it can easily be moved indoors when the weather turns colder. Either way, to get the best out of it, it needs to be in your warmest, sunniest spot all summer long.

When you first plant the tubers out and they're just starting into growth, they need a lot of moisture, so water frequently and deeply. This will encourage the flowers to form. When the plant is in growth, water in some liquid fertiliser every two weeks. Once the main plant has flowered it won't flower again, so you'll need to remove the small offsets that appear on the main plant and grow them on. Plant each offset on into a small pot of fresh compost and keep well watered until growth starts to slow in autumn. If they're going to flower the following year, they need as long a period of growth as possible – ideally at least four weeks – before they start to go into dormancy in autumn. When this happens, the leaves will shrivel and yellow. At this point, slowly reduce watering until the soil is completely dry. Keep it dry throughout winter.

Tuberoses needs warmth – at least 15°C/59°F throughout winter – so a greenhouse that is just frost-free isn't likely to be sufficient. You may be better off overwintering them in the house.

SUPPORTING CAST

There are many stunning, pale plants that aren't night-scented but that deserve a place in the night garden for their shape and purity of colour. I have included several white winter-flowering plants in this section, my idea being that you still need something to lure you out of the house and down the garden in the dead of winter. Some of these are beautifully scented in warm weather, but not particularly on chilly winter nights. Other important plants to consider for the night garden are those with silver leaves. Their metallic sheen reflects even low light; several are low-growing ground-cover plants that create rivers of night-shimmering silver among your other plants. I have also included a few particularly useful coloured plants. These will give your white garden a bit of colour and variety during the day, but will sink back into obscurity come evening.

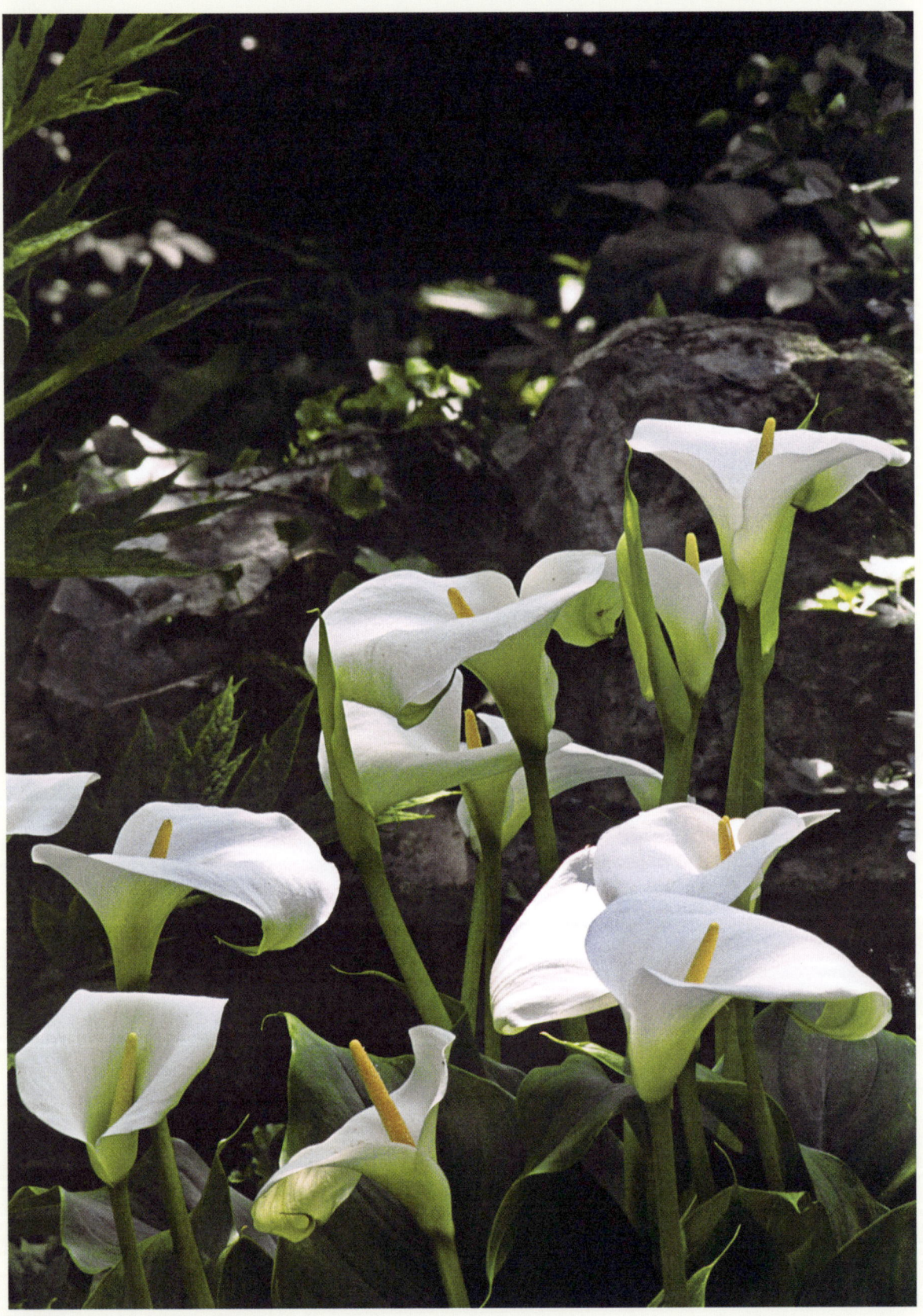

Arum lily

Zantedeschia aethiopica

Situation:	Full sun
Hardiness:	Frost-hardy (USDA zone 9)
Soil type:	Moist or as a marginal aquatic
Height:	90 cm/36 in
Spread:	50cm/20 in
Propagation:	From divisions in spring
Planting:	Plant in spring
Flowering period:	Late spring to midsummer
Toxicity:	Highly toxic

It is not only back gardens that can be turned into twilight gardens. You can also plant up a pond or a bog garden for evening viewing. The moisture-loving herbaceous perennial *Zantedeschia aethiopica* produces fabulous large pure-white spathes – petal-like structures wrapped around the true flowers, which are borne in a spike or 'spadex'. Imagine them appearing to float serenely above a moonlit pond or gently lit from below by a few floating candles. And, when the plant isn't in flower, it has attractive glossy green arrow-shaped leaves, too.

Ideally, this plant needs really damp soil, like that in a bog garden, but you can try growing it in normal garden soil enriched with lots of organic matter such as well-rotted horse manure or garden compost. It is only frost-hardy so it can't tolerate temperatures below −5°C/23°F. In most areas, once the plants have died back, it is a good idea to protect them over winter by applying a thick mulch of bark chippings or similar. They can also be grown as marginal plants in a pond, but will need lifting out over winter.

To propagate them, lift the clump in spring or autumn and split it using a fork or spade. Replant immediately and keep well watered. 'Crowborough' is a cultivar with particularly large white spathes and architectural leaves.

Christmas Rose

Helleborus niger

Situation:	Partial shade
Hardiness:	Hardy (USDA zone 8)
Soil type:	Moist, humus-rich
Height:	30 cm/12 in
Spread:	40 cm/15 in
Propagation:	From divisions or sow seed in spring
Planting:	Plant in spring
Flowering period:	Winter to early spring
Toxicity:	Toxic

Most winter flowers are tiny little things that have taken the evolutionary path of going small to avoid the ravages of winter weather. Hellebores have instead opted to go tough. Their flowers are the biggest of all the winter blooms: they really are quite an impressive size for a winter flower, and that's because their petals (technically 'sepals') are solid and weather-resistant. *Helleborus niger*, the Christmas rose, has pure white petals. Its flowers aren't as pendent (drooping) as some hellebores, which helps them to show up on a dark winter night. They are a great choice for a front garden, where they will greet you cheerily as you get home on cold, dark evenings. This is an evergreen plant and so bears its dark, glossy leaves (all the better to show up the flowers) year-round.

Hellebores are useful plants because they thrive in shade. Ideally the shade should be of the dappled, woodland variety, but they are not hugely fussy. They like a moist, humus-rich soil, so dig in lots of leaf mould or garden compost before planting. You should also spread a thick mulch of leaf mould or compost over the soil every autumn. This not only enriches the soil, but also provides a background that shows the plant off to best advantage when it flowers.

Clematis

Clematis Montana

Situation:	Full sun or partial shade (roots in shade)
Hardiness:	Hardy (USDA zone 8)
Soil type:	Fairly well drained
Height:	7 m/23 ft
Spread:	4 m/13 ft
Propagation:	From cuttings in summer
Planting:	Plant out in early summer
Flowering period:	Late spring
Toxicity:	Non-toxic

This is a huge, vigorous climber that you should plant only where it has space to romp away. But if you have a wall or an ugly outbuilding you want to cover, or a sturdy pergola over which to train it, and you can really let it grow furiously, clematis is a magnificent plant. It is smothered in pale, scented flowers in late spring and into early summer. This mass of pale flowers makes a great backdrop for an evening planting scheme.

Clematis like sunshine but they don't like their roots to be hot, so either plant them where their feet are in the shade and their head is in the sun, or provide some ground-cover planting, such as hardy geraniums, around the base to keep them shaded. You will also need to provide sturdy supports for the plant to climb up. Stretched wires are good against a wall, or you can help them get started clambering up a pergola support by tying the stems in to begin with.

Always plant clematis a few centimetres/inches deeper than the level of the soil in the pot in which you bought it. They suffer from a fungal problem called clematis wilt, in which the stems can suddenly collapse and die. If you have planted your clematis deeply enough, you can simply cut the affected stems right down and more will sprout from below the ground.

Foxglove

Digitalis purpurea f. *albiflora*

Situation:	Partial shade
Hardiness:	Hardy (USDA zone 3)
Soil type:	Humus-rich, well drained
Height:	100cm/40 in
Spread:	5 cm/20 in
Propagation:	Sow seeds in late spring and early summer
Planting:	Plant out where they are to flower in autumn
Flowering period:	Late spring, early summer
Toxicity:	Highly toxic

Although they are not night-scented, white foxgloves send up impressive spires of white flowers that provide a strong vertical accent in an evening garden. *Digitalis purpurea f. albiflora* is pure white and – unlike many other foxgloves – the flowers are entirely unspotted and really glow in low-light conditions. Foxgloves are woodland plants, so they are most at home in dappled sun and well-drained but humus-rich soil. But they are pretty tolerant plants, so it is worth trying them in most soils.

Since these plants are biennials, sow seed in late spring or early summer for flowers the following year. Sow into seed trays filled with seed compost and prick the seedlings out into individual pots once they are large enough to handle. Plant them out in autumn where they are to flower. They die after flowering but self-seed readily, so once they are established you should never be left wanting. Leave the dead plants until spring to give them a chance to drop all their seed, then pull them up and compost them. One of the benefits of this self seeding habit is that the spires pop up throughout the garden and you will find foxgloves in places you might not have thought to plant them. They look great in a cottage-garden border, but work just as well among ferns and other woodland plants.

All parts of foxgloves are highly poisonous, so take care to keep pets and children away from them.

Giant Allium

Allium giganteum

Situation:	Full Sun
Hardiness:	Hardy (USDA Zone 8)
Soil type:	Well drained
Height:	1.5 m/5 ft
Spread:	15 cm/6 in
Propagation:	Lift bulbs in summer and separate offsets to grow on
Planting:	Plant out bulbs in autumn or spring
Flowering period:	Summer
Toxicity:	Toxic

Ornamental onions are an essential ingredient in any cottage garden. The huge, purple, perfectly spherical flower heads of *Allium giganteum* float above the rest of the planting, providing an accent among the more mound-like shapes of many herbaceous perennials. Where they find conditions to their liking, they will multiply and gradually appear throughout your garden. Where the soil is too heavy, however, they will slowly peter out over a few years, and you will have to replant occasionally, just as you would with tulips.

Alliums like a well-drained soil and lots of sun in order to do well. Ideally, you should plant the bulbs in autumn, digging lots of grit into the area first. Don't be tempted just to line each planting hole with grit, however: in wet weather on heavier soils, the grit will simply act as a sump, drawing water from all around. You should plant your alliums at three times their own depth, so a bulb 7.5 cm/3 in across needs to be planted about 23 cm/9 in deep, with its pointed end upwards. They look best planted in groups. Either scatter them in a casually arranged clump or plant them in drifts through and between other plants. For the best flowers, you should feed them with a balanced fertiliser from the moment the leaves appear.

Lamb's Ear 'Silver Carpet'

Stachys byzantina 'Silver Carpet'

Situation:	Full sun
Hardiness:	Hardy (USDA zone 8)
Soil type:	Well drained
Height:	40 cm/15 in
Spread:	60 cm/24 in
Propagation:	Dig up, sever and pot on rooted stems in spring
Planting:	Plant out in spring
Flowering period:	Non-flowering (flowering varieties flower early summer to autumn)
Toxicity:	Non-toxic

Stachys is a ground-cover plant that is great for providing weed-suppressing growth along the front of a border. 'Silver Carpet', with its particularly felty silvery leaves, lives up to its name. The silvery effect is created by thousands of tiny, silky white hairs that cover the leaves. The species is native to Turkey and Iran; the purpose of these hairs is to deflect sunlight in these hot climates, but this reflective quality works equally well in moonlight. 'Silver Carpet' is a non-flowering cultivar, so all of its energy goes into producing its incredibly soft, tactile foliage. Grow it among your white, night scented flowers to provide a silvery background.

All silver-leaved plants prefer a well-drained soil and this one is no exception. If your soil is not naturally sandy or light, mix plenty of grit in and around the planting hole. You should also choose a sunny spot. Thanks to its preference for well-drained soil and its silvery sheen, stachys will look entirely at home in a gravel garden, but it works equally well as an edging plant in a cottage-garden border. You will need to keep the ground around and between the stems weed-free while the plant is getting established, but once it has formed a good, thick mat, it should prevent weeds from germinating.

Lavender

Lavandula angustifolia 'Hidcote'

Situation:	Full sun
Hardiness:	Hardy (USDA zone 8)
Soil type:	Well drained
Height:	60 cm/24 in
Spread:	70 cm/27 in
Propagation:	From cuttings in summer
Planting:	Plant in summer
Flowering period:	Mid- to late summer
Toxicity:	Non-toxic

Lavender has reflective silvery foliage but also produces spikes of flowers in shades ranging from pure white to the deepest purple, so it is a great plant either for creating or complementing an evening planting scheme. *Lavandula angustifolia* 'Hidcote' is a compact lavender often used for hedging because of its ability to keep a good shape. It has particularly pale foliage and contrasting deep purple flowers. Both foliage and flowers are, famously, scented, especially so when they release their volatile oils in the heat of the day. The scent continues a little into the evening, particularly when the plants are handled.

Lavenders suit Mediterranean planting schemes, but also work well as an understorey for roses and other shrubs. They look good in a gravel garden and do well by the sea. They make the perfect edging plant for paths, particularly as they will release their oils when brushed against.

You can treat lavenders in one of two ways: either let them grow all summer and flower in mid- to late summer, then trim them lightly all over; or trim them every now and then all summer to prevent them flowering and to create a piece of lavender topiary. This makes for an unusual and impressive effect. Never prune lavenders back hard and be aware that they are fairly short-lived plants and will eventually need replacing.

Lavender Cotton

Santolina chamaecyparissus

Situation:	Full sun
Hardiness:	Frost-hardy (USDA zone 10)
Soil type:	Well drained
Height:	50 cm/20 in
Spread:	90 cm/36 in
Propagation:	From cuttings in summer
Planting:	Plant out in spring
Flowering period:	Mid- to late summer
Toxicity:	Mildly toxic

Lavender cotton, the common name for *Santolina chamaecyparissus,* grows into a neat, dome-like mound of greyish-green foliage topped with hundreds of little button-like flowers on long stalks. It is an extremely neat plant with a pleasing habit and shape, and it will add an unusual texture to a planting scheme of Mediterranean plants. The pale yellow flowers show up well in the dark, as do the slightly silvery leaves and stems. The aromatic foliage produces its strongest scent during the heat of the day, but it continues to exude scent into the evening and is particularly noticeable if you are passing close by.

The trick is to plant lavender cotton in well-drained soil in full sun. In shadier spots, it is likely to become leggy; in damp soil it may rot. Ordinary garden soil is perfectly adequate: anything richer can lead to leggy growth and disease. Just work in plenty of grit before planting. You can treat this purely as a foliage plant – almost as a piece of topiary – by trimming it back frequently throughout the year to keep a really neat shape and discourage flowering. Alternatively, trim back into the current year's growth after the flowers have faded. In winter, protect the stems with a thick mulch.

Lily of the Valley

Convallaria majalis

Situation:	Shade
Hardiness:	Hardy (USDA zone 8)
Soil type:	Moist, humus-rich
Height:	25cm/10 in
Spread:	30 cm/12 in
Propagation:	Dig up rhizomes in autumn
Planting:	Divide and replant
Flowering period:	Late spring
Toxicity:	Highly toxic

Lily of the valley is a plant that signals the turning of the seasons from spring to summer. Its rich, sweet scent is well loved and, although it is not especially night-scented, its beautiful little dangling, bell-like flowers are pure white and will brighten up a gloomy corner early in the year. The leaves are wide and dark green and the racemes of white flowers tinted with green show up well against this background.

Lily of the valley isn't a dainty thing to be planted among other delicate spring beauties. Truth be told, it is a bit of a thug; you should plant it only where it has room to spread without bothering other plants.

Ideally, it wants a moist, humus-rich soil that mirrors that of its woodland habitat, so dig in plenty of leaf mould or garden compost before planting. An alternative is to grow it in pots for early flowers. Plant the 'pips' (as the small plants are called) in pots in spring and leave them in a greenhouse or cold frame. The extra heat and protection this affords forces them into early growth and flower. You can then treat them as temporary house plants and bring them indoors to enjoy their scent. Place them outside again as soon as the flowers have faded. If you are treating them this way, you will need to remove them from the pots, divide them and replant each year.

Marguerite Daisy

Argyranthemum frutescens

Situation:	Full Sun
Hardiness:	Half-hardy (USDA zone 10)
Soil type:	Well drained
Height:	60 cm/24 in
Spread:	60 cm/24 in
Flowering period:	Early summer to early autumn
Propagation:	From cuttings in spring or summer
Planting:	Plant out in late spring or early summer
Toxicity:	Non-toxic

Marguerites are real powerhouses of summer-flower production. Often sold as bedding plants, they are far more sophisticated than your average blowsy, brightly coloured thing. They form a neat mound of bright green, finely cut leaves and produce big daisy-like flowers all summer long. You may also find them sold as standards or lollipops – balls of foliage on top of straight stems. A pair of these looks great either side of a door or pathway, their pure white flowers glowing in the dark. There are varieties that have very pretty yellow or pink flowers, but these won't show up so well at night. Plant marguerites in well-drained soil or in containers in a mixture of grit and multi-purpose compost. They make useful bedding plants for seaside gardens as they are tolerant of salt and winds, but generally speaking they are not particularly hardy. In milder areas they may survive the winter, but you should cover their base with a thick mulch to protect them from the hardest frosts. In colder areas, you will need to overwinter them in an unheated greenhouse or a porch from autumn onwards. Plants that get frosted at the tips may grow back from their base in spring, but as a precaution against loss, take cuttings in summer and overwinter them carefully.

Meadow cranesbill, 'Mrs Kendall Clark'

Geranium pratense

Situation:	Full sun or partial shade
Hardiness:	Hardy (USDA zone 8)
Soil type:	Any
Height:	90 cm/36 in
Spread:	60 cm/24 in
Propagation:	From divisions in spring or autumn
Planting:	Replant immediately after flowering
Flowering period:	Early to midsummer, sometimes with a second flush
Toxicity:	Non-toxic

If you are looking for a dependable plant with masses of colourful flowers to accompany your pale night-bloomers, you could do worse than to plant a hardy geranium. These low-growing, weed-smothering plants get covered in flowers in shades of purple, pink or white – ideal for complementing the pale, cool colours of a garden planted for the evening. Some have such pale flowers that they show up in the dark themselves; alternatively, you can use darker-flowered cultivars for a splash of daytime colour.

'Mrs Kendall Clark' falls somewhere between the two, as it has greyish-pink flowers with attractive white patterning. It blooms fairly early in the summer, but can be encouraged to produce a second flush if the whole plant is trimmed back by about a third just after the flowers have faded. For a more intense colour, choose *Geranium* 'Ann Folkard', which produces vibrant magenta flowers throughout summer and autumn. For a paler flower, consider *Geranium clarkei* 'Kashmir White', which produces white flowers with delicate pink veining all summer. If you trim these back after flowering, they will form a small, neat mound of leaves. Split plants in spring or autumn every few years to propagate them and to keep them healthy.

Mexican Orange Blossom

Choisya ternata

Hardiness:	Full sun
Soil type:	Hardy (USDA zone 8)
Height:	2.5m/8 ft
Spread:	2.5m/8 ft
Propagation:	From cuttings in spring or summer
Planting:	Plant out in late spring or early summer
Flowering period:	Spring, summer and autumn
Toxicity:	Non-toxic

This luxuriously glossy-leaved, neat shrub would be worth growing just for its lustrous evergreen foliage, but in spring, and then later again in summer, it is covered in starry white flowers with a scent of orange blossom; hence the plant's common name. The scent isn't particularly strong at night, but the flowers look beautiful in the evening light and will scent your garden during the day. *Choisya ternata* 'Sundance' has glossy pale green, almost yellow leaves and the same flowers as the species. Both plants naturally form a compact, mounded shape.

These are hardy shrubs, but they aren't actually the toughest, so they are best suited to gardens in milder areas or to sheltered, sunny corners in colder areas. Plant them in well-drained soil in full sun. Occasionally choisyas may be damaged by hard frosts. If this happens, you can prune them hard and they will produce a new flush of stems. Pruning back the flowered shoots by about 25 cm/10 in after the spring flush will keep the shrub bushy and dense and will encourage a later flush of flowers in summer and autumn.

These plants are good in a low-maintenance garden and, because they can put up with a degree of neglect, are a particularly good choice for a front garden.

Mock Orange

Philadelphus 'Beauclerk'

Situation:	Full sun or partial shade
Hardiness:	Hardy (USDA zone 8)
Soil type:	Fairly well drained
Height:	2.5 m/8 ft
Spread:	2.5 m/8 ft
Propagation:	From cuttings in summer, autumn or winter
Planting:	Plant out in spring or autumn
Flowering period:	Midsummer
Toxicity:	Non-toxic

Philadelphus is a shrub that has all the exuberance of summer. It blooms once a year in midsummer and pretty briefly, it must be admitted, but the flowers are large, white and fragrant. They are not especially night-scented – the plant's aim is to attract day-flying pollinators rather than night-flying ones – but they bring a strong orange-blossom scent to the garden by day – and by night they positively glow.

Philadelphus 'Beauclerk' has an arching habit that produces a fountain of impressive white flowers with slightly pink-flushed centres. To make the most of the fountain-like effect, plant it in a spot where it will have plenty of room to shoot out its flower sprays, otherwise the effect will be ruined. Pruning is simple; after it has finished flowering, cut about a third of the oldest stems out completely, right down to the ground.

You may question whether it is worth making space for a shrub that flowers so briefly, but you can extend its season of interest by growing a climber through it, such as a small clematis. It looks good in a shrub border or at the back of a cottage-garden border. There are many cultivars to choose from, including the compact *P.* 'Manteau de Hermine' and the yellow-leaved *P. coronarius* 'Aureus'.

Peony

Paeonia 'Claire de Lune'

Situation:	Full sun or partial shade
Hardiness:	Hardy (USDA zone 7)
Soil type:	Rich, moist and fertile but well drained
Height:	80 cm/30 in
Spread:	70 cm/ 27 in
Propagation:	From divisions in autumn or early spring
Planting:	Plant out in spring or autumn
Flowering period:	Late spring to midsummer
Toxicity:	Non-toxic

Peonies defy rational gardening logic. They flower for an extremely brief spell, making a glorious statement in the garden for a short while, and look fairly dull for the rest of the year. But what flowers they produce! They are always big and impressively luxurious, and they are always a talking point. Peonies are one of those flowers that you just have to take a deep breath and plant – the horticultural equivalent of buying yourself the occasional expensive pair of shoes.

They are hungry plants, and won't tolerate mean conditions, so you should plant them in a really humus-rich soil that retains moisture well yet allows excess water to drain away. Mulch thickly with well-rotted manure or garden compost once a year to ensure the soil stays rich. Remove dead flowers after they have faded and remove any foliage that looks spotted: this is the first signs of botrytis.

'Claire de Lune' has an unusual flower. It is huge, single and with sweet-scented pale yellow petals, but the centre is made up of a great many golden yellow stamens, so it looks like a fluffy golden ball. The flowers show up well in moonlight (hence the name), but if you can't find this cultivar, there are many other pale yellow, pale pink and white-flowered peonies to choose from, many of them scented.

Purple Coneflower

Echinacea purpurea

Situation:	Full sun or partial shade
Hardiness:	Hardy
Soil type:	Humus-rich
Height:	80 cm/30 in
Spread:	30 cm/12 in
Propagation:	From divisions in sprint or autumn
Planting:	Dig, split and replant where you want to grow
Flowering period:	Mid- to late summer
Toxicity:	Non-toxic

Echinaceas provide late-summer colour in perennial borders. While not really night plants – although there are pure white cultivars such as 'White Swan' that show up well in evening planting – they are included here since they rub along very nicely with other cottage garden perennials or in a mixed border. Plus, they will extend the season of interest in your garden into late summer and autumn, and even into winter. Once the petals have faded, the central cone stays on the plant a long time, providing a strong winter shape that is particularly pleasing after a hoar frost.

Echinaceas do well in most sunny or slightly shaded spots, but ideally they like a fertile soil and hate having permanently damp roots. To achieve this, mix organic matter and some grit into the soil when planting to ensure the soil is fertile and evenly moist but not too damp. They don't like having their roots disturbed, so only lift and divide after a good few years. Lift the plant in spring or autumn, shake the soil off, then use a sharp knife to divide the clump, ensuring each piece has some root and stem. Replant and keep well watered. They usually self-seed fairly freely so you shouldn't need to divide them purely for propagation, only to keep them healthy.

Purple Top

Verbena bonariensis

Situation:	Full sun
Hardiness:	Frost-hardy (USDA zone 8)
Soil type:	Moist but well drained
Height:	1.5 m/5 ft
Spread:	45 cm/18 in
Propagation:	Sow seed in autumn or spring
Planting:	Plant in spring
Flowering period:	Midsummer to autumn
Toxicity:	Non-toxic

Verbena bonariensis is a plant that drifts through other plantings. It has tall, wiry stems topped with little heads of small purple flowers. One of the pleasures of this plant is that it is almost transparent so you can plant it anywhere in a border – even at the front – without blocking out the view of the plants behind. It will self-seed freely if it likes the conditions, so you will end up with plants all through your borders as well as popping up in cracks in patios and paths.

Verbena is a perfectly lovely purple in the daytime and will blend in with all manner of colour schemes, from hot and fiery to cool and pastel. I have included it here because of what it does in the evening. Just as other purple flowers start to fade into the gloom, the flowers of *V. bonariensis* begin to glow. It is almost as if a little light has been switched on inside each one, providing pinpricks of bright purple scattered throughout the garden. They are quite a sight. Of course, they eventually disappear into the darkness and only the true whites remain, glowing away, but this verbena more than earns its keep in the early evening garden.

In some areas, this verbena can prove slightly tender, so you should cover the crowns with a thick mulch over winter. You will usually have enough new seedlings scattered about, however, to make up for any winter losses.

Rose

Rosa 'Madame Hardy';

Rosa 'Climbing Iceberg'

Situation:	Full sun
Hardiness:	Hardy (USDA zone 3)
Soil type:	Humus-rich
Height:	2 m/6 ft 6 in
Spread:	1 m/3 ft 3 in
Propagation:	From cuttings in spring or autumn
Planting:	Plant out in winter
Flowering period:	Early to late summer
Toxicity:	Non-toxic

Roses are no more scented in the evening than they are in the day, but they do add an additional gentle scent to the garden at night, and a floriferous white rose, covering a fence or wall, is a glorious sight in the evening.

'Madame Hardy' is a damask rose and an old French variety. This is the one to go for if you want a short-lived blast of strong, delicious scent in early summer at the height of the rose season. 'Iceberg' blooms throughout the summer and into early autumn, but the scent isn't quite so magnificent. The choice is yours – or perhaps you have room in your garden for both.

Roses love a really rich soil and do particularly well in clay that has been improved with plenty of well-rotted horse manure or garden compost. You can grow them in sandier soils, too, but they are never quite so good. Whatever the soil, mulch regularly once a year. Feed regularly from early spring onwards with a high-potash fertiliser, such as tomato feed, to encourage flowering.

Climbers need to be carefully trained and pruned if they are not to shoot straight to the top of the support and flower only where passing birds can enjoy them. Provide a sturdy trellis or series of wires to support them. Try to tie the shoots into as horizontal a position as you can, to encourage more flowers. Do this when pruning, and again throughout summer as long as whippy growths appear. Prune in autumn or winter, removing the oldest stems completely and reducing side shoots that have flowered by two-thirds.

ABOVE: Choose old-fashioned, pale-coloured or white roses and they will glow in the low light of the evening while scenting your garden.

THE TWILIGHT GARDENER

Rosemary

Rosmarinus officinalis

Situation:	Full sun
Hardiness:	Hardy (USDA zone 8)
Soil type:	Well drained
Height:	1.5 cm/5 ft
Spread:	1.5 cm/½ in
Propagation:	From cuttings in summer
Planting:	Plant out in spring
Flowering period:	Early spring to midsummer
Toxicity:	Non-toxic

Rosemary is an aromatic Mediterranean shrub with greyish-green, slightly silvery leaves. It makes a good background plant for a scheme of other silver-leaved Mediterranean plants and also looks good among herbaceous perennials. It is evergreen and therefore looks good all winter when other plants have died back or lost their leaves. It also produces purple-blue flowers over an extremely long period, starting early in spring. This makes it a useful plant for wildlife, providing nectar for early-flying bees and other insects at a time when supplies are low.

Treat rosemary as you would any other silver-leaved Mediterranean plant: it wants a well-drained soil and plenty of sun. If the soil is too rich, it is likely to become leggy, and in damp soils there may be some rotting off. But it is a little more tolerant and hardier than many other silver-leaved plants.

Like all silver-leaved plants, rosemary is likely to die if you cut it back hard, but it does get leggy with age. You can put this off for a while by trimming it back lightly into the young growth every year after the first flush of flowers has faded. However, it's generally considered short-lived. After a few years, it will start to show its age, becoming woody and gappy. There's not much you can do then but replace it.

Sage

Salvia officinalis 'Tricolor'

Situation:	Full sun or very light shade
Hardiness:	Hardy (USDA zone 8)
Soil type:	Well drained
Height:	1 m/3 ft 3 in
Spread:	1 m/3 ft 3 in
Propagation:	From cuttings in spring or early summer
Planting:	Plant out in spring
Flowering period:	Early summer
Toxicity:	Non-toxic

Salvia officinalis 'Tricolor' is a very pretty, aromatic Mediterranean herb. It has greyish-green foliage edged in cream and the tips of the growths are tinged with purple. I have included sage as a night garden plant because the variegation of the leaves helps it to show up in the dark.

Hailing from the Mediterranean, sage needs well-drained soil and sun, although it can take a little light shade.

In summer, sage will produce spikes of lilac-blue flowers; you will get a better-shaped plant and nicer leaves if you prevent it from flowering by regularly nipping out the top few leaves. This keeps the plant bushy and produces lots of fresh purple-flushed new leaves. Sage, along with other silver-leaved plants, doesn't take kindly to being pruned hard, so this constant nipping out is essential to keep the plant in good shape.

These plants are usually grown for their aromatic foliage. You can use it in cooking – in traditional stuffings, in pork or chicken recipes and in sage oils for pasta dishes – just like the plain-leaved sage. Sage plants are short-lived sub-shrubs and will need replacing after five or six years.

Sicilian Chamomile

Anthemis cupaniana

Situation:	Full sun
Hardiness:	Hardy (USDA zone 5)
Soil type:	Well drained
Height:	30 cm/12 in
Spread:	90 cm/ 36 in
Propagation:	Sow seed in spring
Planting:	Plant out in late early summer
Flowering period:	Early to late summer
Toxicity:	Non-toxic

Sicilian chamomile is the perfect ground-cover or front-of-border plant for a moonlight garden. It has delicately cut silver foliage that creeps along the ground, forming a carpet that spills over the edges of paths, softening them gently. The leaves are at their most silver in summer and glint metallically on moonlit nights. In summer, this carpet of foliage is covered with a mass of small daisy-like flowers that keep their colour and freshness for a long time. In winter, the leaves turn greener but remain on the plant. The foliage is aromatic when crushed, which is another reason to use it by a path where it might occasionally be trodden on accidentally.

This is a plant for well-drained soils and looks good in a gravel garden. In heavier soils, mix plenty of grit around the planting hole when you plant. This chamomile will spread fairly quickly, but you can easily keep it neat. Trim the flowers off as soon as they fade to encourage a second flush, then trim again later on and a little harder to keep the plant small and bushy. The trimming will stimulate shoots lower down and so prevent legginess. Alternatively, you can leave the second flush of flowers to set seed, then the plant will seed itself freely around the garden.

Silver Feather

Gonospermum ptarmiciflorum

Situation:	Full sun
Hardiness:	Half-hardy (USDA zone 11)
Soil type:	Well drained, sandy
Height:	50 cm/ 20 in
Spread:	40 cm/15 in
Propagation:	Sow seeds in early spring or take cuttings in summer
Planting:	Plant out in spring
Flowering period:	Late summer
Toxicity:	Non-toxic

The extreme silver, almost white, finely cut feather-like leaves of *Gonospermum ptarmiciflorum* make it shine out in low light. But this is not a very hardy plant and it is most often grown as an annual foliage filler for bedding schemes. In hanging baskets and containers it makes the perfect foil for white flowers. For moonlight garden bedding, team it with white petunias and you will have a magically pale, silvery scheme that is also night-scented.

These plants like well-drained compost and will tolerate a little drought – a trait that makes them even better candidates for hanging baskets or pots, as these often get neglected at some point over the summer. When you are planting them, mix some grit or vermiculite into the compost for good drainage.

They do produce yellow flowers later in the summer, but the trick is not to let them flower. Pinch out the tips occasionally throughout the summer and you will keep the plant small and bushy and force it to produce young, fresh-looking growth instead of growing large and leggy. It is a little tricky to keep these plants going from year to year, but you can take cuttings in summer and overwinter them in a cool greenhouse. Otherwise, grow from seed in early spring or buy small plants in mid-spring.

Smooth Hydrangea

Hydrangea arborescens 'Annabelle'

Situation:	Sun or partial shade
Hardiness:	Hardy (USDA zone 8)
Soil type:	Moist, humus-rich, but well drained
Height:	2 m/6 ft 6 in
Spread:	2 m/6 ft 6 in
Propagation:	From cuttings in summer
Planting:	Plant in early summer
Flowering period:	Early summer to early autumn
Toxicity:	Toxic

Hydrangeas have a reputation for being slightly naff and suburban, but they are wonderfully dependable, fuss-free plants that produce masses of huge flowers throughout summer. Personally, I love the coloured ones, but if you are a bit squeamish about having them in your garden, you should still consider making room for 'Annabelle'. It is an extremely classy plant that even the most fashion-conscious gardener couldn't turn their nose up at. It produces small green globes of buds that turn into huge, pure-white footballs – great for looming out from the far reaches of your night garden. In autumn, these become architectural seed heads that stay on the plant all winter and glisten in the frost.

These are easy, hardy plants that don't take a great deal of looking after once they are established. Plant them in spring or autumn in a sunny or partially shaded spot, water them until they are established – and that's it. These plants will survive drought (although they produce smaller flowers in drier soils) and aren't bothered by cold. Each spring, remove the tips of the stems back to the first shooting bud and remove any dead stems right back to their base. Apart from that, a hydrangea shouldn't need much in the way of pruning unless it gets too large. If that happens, cut back about a third of the oldest stems each spring, right back to their base.

Snowdrop

Galanthus nivalis

Situation:	Partial shade
Hardiness:	Hardy (USDA zone 8)
Soil type:	Humus-rich
Height:	10 cm/4 in
Spread:	10 cm/4in
Propagation:	Lift and split clumps and replant sections
Planting:	Just after flowering in winter
Flowering period:	Winter
Toxicity:	Toxic

Chances are you won't be spending a great deal of time in the garden on mid- and late-winter nights, but it is good to have something to lure you out there. Otherwise, if you are out of the house all day, you are unlikely to see much of your garden at all during the winter months. A few pale-coloured winter plants may just tempt you away from the cosy fire and television for a few minutes. The ultimate pale coloured winter plant has to be the snowdrop. *Galanthus nivalis* is the common snowdrop. You can buy them in their hundreds at a very reasonable price and scatter them throughout the garden. As they need constant moisture, they are best planted 'in the green' rather than as bulbs. When you buy bulbs, there is a risk that they will have dried out, which means they are likely to come up 'blind' – that is, they won't flower for at least the first year. Use them en masse to create a carpet under deciduous shrubs and trees, or in little clumps among other plants. They are woodland plants and so prefer a moist, humus-rich soil and partial shade – the shade of trees is perfect. Planting time is just after flowering time.

Tulip

Tulipa 'White Triumphator'

Situation:	Full sun
Hardiness:	Hardy (USDA zone 8)
Soil type:	Well drained
Height:	60 cm /24 in
Spread:	15 cm/6 in
Propagation:	Lift bulbs in summer and separate offsets to grow on
Planting:	Or just plant new bulbs in autumn
Flowering period:	Late spring
Toxicity:	Toxic

Tulips appear at a time when the evenings are getting lighter and warmer and you may just be starting to spend a little extra time outside, pottering around weeding and getting your garden in order for the summer days to come. 'White Triumphator' is a particularly elegant tulip, tall and stately with pure white, curved petals. A few groups of these around your garden on a warm, late spring evening will be sure to lure you out of the house with a glass of wine in your hand.

There are only very few situations where you can throw tulips in the ground and depend on them to come back year after year. They like really well-drained soil and a sunny position, so if you can provide a spot where they are guaranteed to get a baking each summer and not sit in damp soil through the winter, they may last quite a long time.

In such spots, be sure to plant them extra deep. Plant them in late autumn, as this helps to keep them going. On heavier soils, they will simply fade away and the flowering will be greatly reduced even in the second year from planting.

Many people lift their tulips after the leaves have faded, store them somewhere dry for the winter, then replant them in autumn. Others simply buy fresh bulbs each year. This is really the only way to guarantee a great display, but it is rather extravagant.

Winter Honeysuckle

Lonicera fragrantissima

Situation:	Full sun or partial shade
Hardiness:	Hardy (USDA zone 8)
Soil type:	Humus-rich
Height:	2 m/6 ft 6 in
Spread:	2.5 m/8 ft
Propagation:	From cuttings in summer
Planting:	Plant out in spring or autumn
Flowering period:	Late winter or early spring
Toxicity:	Mildly toxic

Many winter-flowering shrubs are scented, although not especially night-scented. There are few night-flying insects around on winter nights and it is pretty hard work attracting any pollinators in the depths of winter without becoming a specialist gardener. But shrubs such as *Hamamelis*, *Viburnum x bodnantense* and *Lonicera fragrantissima* are worth growing for their daytime scent, while *L. fragrantissima* is also useful for the evening garden. Its arching sprays of pink-tinged white flowers will stand out on dark winter nights and may even tempt you down to the far reaches of the garden to catch a waft of their spring-like lemony scent.

This plant is a shrubby honeysuckle and has little in common, habit-wise, with the climbing honeysuckle. It does, however, share the climber's ability to produce a wonderful fragrance. It will grow in sun or partial shade, but you will get a better display of flowers if it is grown in full sun. Plant in evenly moist but not wet soil that has been enriched with plenty of organic matter. Pruning to keep it within bounds always makes this plant look a little awkward, so try to plant it where it will have plenty of room to spread out. If the branches become congested, remove up to a third of them each year, right back to their base.

BACKSTAGE BEAUTIES

Not all your plants need to be showy and glitzy. Some have to do the hard work, providing the garden with backbone and solidity. These are the trees, shrubs and hedges. You might use some of these plants in any garden, but there are certain backbone plants that are particularly good at night. Some are silvery or white, such as the silver birch or the weeping pear, both of which will glint away in even the lowest light. Others, such as yew, are particularly dense and dark. They are ideal for throwing the whites and pales into sharp relief.

Hedging plants are particularly important in evening gardens. They filter wind and help create an enclosed, sheltered space that slows the movement of air and keeps night-time scents trapped close by. Some hedging plants also work extremely well as topiary, which can be interspersed among your pale, ephemeral beauties to provide strong structural effects. I have also included several plants here for their dramatic or craggy silhouettes, which will provide an arresting outline against the night sky.

Apple

Malus domestica

Situation:	Full sun
Hardiness:	Hardy (USDA zone 8)
Soil type:	Moist, well drained
Height:	From 1 m/3 ft 3 in to 4m/13 ft, depending on rootstock
Spread:	1 m/3 ft to 4.5m/13 8 in, depending on rootstock
Propagation:	From bud grafts in winter
Planting:	Plant out in autumn or winter
Flowering period:	Late summer to autumn
Toxicity:	Non-toxic

Every garden should contain a fruit tree or two. Apple trees have wonderfully craggy outlines and a large specimen can create a fine silhouette against the night sky or at the back of a border. If you have a small garden, choose a smaller variety: it will still lend a garden maturity within a few years. In spring, just as the evenings are getting lighter, the trees are covered in beautiful white and pink blossom. There are few more reliable crops than apples and, come late summer and autumn, a mature tree will produce armfuls of fruit.

Choosing the correct-sized plant for your garden is easy since apple trees are grafted onto a number of different rootstocks. The rootstock determines the rate of growth. M27 is the tiniest and the one to choose for pots, growing to just 1 m/3 ft 3 in by 1 m/3 ft 3 in. M9 reaches 1.9 m/6 ft 3 in by 1.9 m/6 ft 3 in; M26 1.8 m/5 ft 10 in by 2.3 m/7 ft 6 in; MM106 3 m/9 ft 9 in by 3.6 m/11 ft 9 in; and MM111 4 m/13 ft by 4.5 m/14 ft 6 in.

The smaller-growing plants produce fruit sooner, but the larger plants produce more fruit once they are established. Apple trees need another pollinating tree nearby in order to fruit well, so you may need to plant at least two of them, although there may be a pollinating tree in a neighbouring garden.

Bay Tree

Laurus nobilis

Situation:	Full sun or partial shade
Hardiness:	Frost-hardy (USDA zone 10)
Soil type:	Fairly moist with good drainage
Height:	12 m/39 ft 4in
Spread:	9 m/29 ft 6 in
Propagation:	Sow seed in autumn or take cuttings in summer
Planting:	Plant out in spring or autumn
Flowering period:	Spring
Toxicity:	Non-toxic

Left unpruned, bay can make a huge evergreen plant and could even be considered a pretty good backdrop for a pale planting scheme, but it is more often shaped into topiary and most often into a lollipop – a sphere of foliage balanced on top of a straight stem. In this guise, bay can provide a point of structure and solidity among floatier, paler, night-scented flowers.

You can buy bay trees ready-trained or you can train your own. If you are training your own, look for a young plant with a straight stem. If you can't find one, cut all the growth back in early spring to encourage a flush of fresh, straight stems, then you can select the most promising and cut the rest right back to the ground. Push a bamboo cane into the soil close to the stem and tie the stem to it as it grows. When it has reached the desired height for the top of your lollipop, nip out the tip. Branches will start to grow from just below this point. You should also completely remove any side shoots that emerge from the main stem. It will take a few years, but gradually the lollipop head will fill out and the plant can take its place in the garden.

Beech

Fagus sylvatica

Situation:	Full sun or partial shade
Hardiness:	Hardy (USDA zone 8)
Soil type:	Well drained
Height:	23 m/75 ft if left unpruned
Spread:	18 m/59 ft if left unpruned
Propagation:	Sow seed in autumn
Planting:	Plant out in autumn or winter
Flowering period:	Spring
Toxicity:	Toxic to dogs

Beech makes a wonderful hedge. It is not particularly dark or dense, unlike evergreen yew, but it has a charm of its own. You should definitely consider it as a backdrop to a night-time border, particularly where the soil is sandy.

Beech has fairly large leaves compared to yew, and isn't evergreen. But the beauty of beech is that its leaves turn a gorgeous coppery colour in autumn, which then cling to the plant all winter, so you get the privacy and all-year-round cover of an evergreen as well as seasonal change. The leaves finally fall in spring as the fresh green folds of the new leaves appear all over the hedge.

Beech does like well-drained soil, so don't try to plant it anywhere remotely boggy. This makes it a particularly useful hedging plant for dryer areas and anywhere affected by drought. Dig out a trench the length of the hedge and backfill with a mixture of organic matter and soil before planting. To make sure the beech gets well established, it is best to plant bare-rooted plants in winter.

Trimming the hedge regularly to keep it relatively small helps it retain its leaves over winter. To achieve the best leaf retention, trim in fairly late summer.

Black Bamboo

Phyllostachys nigra

Situation:	Full sun or partial shade
Hardiness:	Hardy (USDA zone 8)
Soil type:	Moist, well drained
Height:	4 m/14 ft
Spread:	3 m/9 ft 9 in
Propagation:	Dig up, remove small chunks in spring then replant
Planting:	Plant any time
Flowering period:	Non-flowering
Toxicity:	Non-toxic

As well as creating a dark, mysterious backdrop against which white and pale flowers can glow, *Phyllostachys nigra* or black bamboo, has the added benefit of being a noisy plant. Admittedly, the noises are subtle – the swishing of the papery leaves and the knocking together of the woody stems – but subtle noises like these (the trickle of a fountain is another one) create a sense of atmosphere and help to block out extraneous sounds, like the noise of traffic or the hum of neighbours' voices. This is particularly important if you plan to use your garden for relaxation and quiet time, since it helps to focus your attention within.

P. nigra is a clumping bamboo, which means there is no danger of it running amok across your garden. It has fresh green leaves and glossy culms (the name given to the stems) of the deepest black. The culms emerge pale green in spring and turn black over the summer. To display them at their best and to emphasise their glossiness, thin out the oldest shoots and remove all the green growth to about one-third of the way up the stem. You can polish them, too, if you have time on your hands.

Cabbage Palm
Cordyline australis

Situation:	Full sun
Hardiness:	Frost-hardy (USDA zone 10)
Soil type:	Well drained
Height:	5 m/16 ft 4 in
Spread:	3 m/9 ft 9 in
Propagation:	Sow seeds in spring or remove pot up suckers in spring
Planting:	Plant in spring
Flowering period:	Summer
Toxicity:	Mildly toxic

Cordyline is a stylish addition to any garden, if the climate is mild enough for it to grow large. It forms a central stem from which arching, strap-like leaves with pointed ends emanate. When it is small, cordyline can be used as a centrepiece for a bedding arrangement or it can simply be planted in a pot. In milder areas, you can try planting it in a border and seeing how it fares, but choose the plain green species as this is hardier than the variegated or red-leaved cultivars. If conditions permit, it can grow into a large, substantial plant with a spectacularly spiky silhouette; if it's happy, it will send out branches. I have included it here because it makes such a wonderful silhouette plant for the back of a night-time border.

In colder areas, you may have to keep it in a pot and move it into a cold greenhouse or porch each winter. Alternatively, try leaving it outdoors and protecting it with a swathe of horticultural fleece over the winter. Even in milder areas, the leaves can get battered by winds. Some people tie the leaves together to stop this from happening, but this looks quite ugly and isn't really necessary.

Chusan Palm

Trachycarpus fortunei

Situation:	Full sun
Hardiness:	Frost-hardy (USDA zone 10)
Soil type:	Well drained
Height:	10 m/32 ft 9 in
Spread:	2.5 m/8ft 2 in
Propagation:	Sow seeds in spring or autumn in a heated propogator
Planting:	Plant in spring
Flowering period:	Early summer
Toxicity:	Non-toxic

Trachycarpus is a plant that works beautifully in the night garden, creating a dramatic outline against the sky. Commonly known as the Chusan or windmill palm, it is one of the hardiest palms, so if you want to create a subtropical effect in a temperate garden, this is the one to try. It slowly forms a thick trunk covered in coarse, brown fibres that make it look hairy. At the top of the trunk it produces huge, palmate, fan-shaped leaves that stay on the plant year-round, providing valuable structure in winter. It grows slowly when young, but can grow as much as 30 cm/12 in a year once it is established. If you want to keep it small, grow it in a pot.

While trachycarpus likes a well-drained soil and will tolerate any soil except one that is permanently moist (it doesn't appreciate sitting in water over the winter), it will put on its best growth where there is adequate moisture. Once established, it will also tolerate drought. A sunny or partially shaded spot is best, but the most important thing to remember when choosing a site is that it needs shelter from winds. The plant will grow fine but when the leaves are battered about, they start to look brown and tatty.

Crab Apple

Malus × zumi 'Golden Hornet'

Situation:	Full sun or dappled shade
Hardiness:	Hardy (USDA zone 8)
Soil type:	Moist, well drained
Height:	10 m/32 ft 9 in
Spread:	9 m/29 ft 6 in
Propagation:	From grafts in winter
Planting:	Plant out in autumn or winter
Flowering period:	Spring
Toxicity:	Non-toxic

Crab apples have the same craggy outline as apple trees. Their fruits are extremely decorative and stay on the tree much longer than normal apples – unless, of course, you pick them and eat them. *Malus x zumi* 'Golden Hornet' is included here for its lovely outline, although it offers other delights too. In spring, the fat pink buds become a profusion of blowsy white blossom, while in autumn the tree is smothered in bright yellow fruits. These light up your garden of an autumn dusk, hanging like Christmas baubles long after the leaves have dropped and well into winter.

These trees want the same conditions as apple trees – good, rich soil and full sun. However, since you don't need the fruits to ripen fully, they will tolerate a little light and dappled shade. Ideally, you shouldn't prune your crab apple much: they look better when they are allowed to grow naturally. If the centre of the plant becomes congested, it can lead to fungal problems from a lack of airflow. When that happens, it's best to prune. Do so in early summer, before the following year's flower buds have started to form, by cutting back any stems that cross in the middle to create an open, cup-shaped tree.

Heavenly Bamboo

Nandina domestica

Situation:	Sun or partial shade
Hardiness:	Hardy (USDA zones 4-10)
Soil type:	Rich, moist soil; likes acid soil but will tolerate others
Height:	2 m/6 ft 6 in
Spread:	1 m/3 ft 3 in
Propagation:	Dig up and pot on runners
Planting:	Plant out in autumn
Flowering period:	Summer
Toxicity:	Berries are toxic

Nandina domestica is known as the heavenly bamboo. In fact, it isn't a true bamboo at all, but it fulfils a similar role in the evening garden by adding to the plant noises that help create a feeling of enclosure and distance from the outside world. Nandina leaves make a kind of papery rustling as the wind blows over it or as you run your hands through it (the papery texture makes it hard to resist touching it, too). Where it differs from most bamboos is in the fineness of its stems and its size. It grows to only around 2 m (6 ft 6 in) in height, making it useful for small gardens and suitable for a large pot.

Nandina's evergreen leaves change colour throughout the year, with new shoots a pinkish-coral, turning green, and then shades of red and orange in autumn. It holds onto those leaves all winter. Plumes of white flowers are produced in summer, and occasionally you may get a few red berries in winter too. Once planted and established, this is a plant that produces a great show yet needs very little care and attention: it is the perfect plant for a low-maintenance garden.

Himalayan Birch

Betula utilis subsp. *jacquemontii*

Situation:	Full sun or dappled shade
Hardiness:	Hardy (USDA zone 8)
Soil type:	Moist, well drained
Height:	Up to 18m/59 ft
Spread:	Up to 9m/29 ft 6 in
Propagation:	From grafts in winter
Planting:	Plant out in autumn
Flowering period:	Catkins in spring
Toxicity:	Non-toxic

Silver birch has pure white stems that provide a ghostly outline in the night garden. A group of several of them is an impressive sight, particularly if they are planted close together. They look good in winter, when the leaves have fallen and the bark is revealed in all its glory. They are also great for providing a truly dramatic backdrop to a garden planted for an evening use.

Betula utilis var. jacquemontii, the Himalayan birch, has even whiter bark than silver birch. It is the most popular and widely available of the really white-stemmed birches, but others are even whiter. *B. u. var. jacquemontii* 'Grayswood Ghost' has possibly the palest bark of all. Over time, the bark will start to get a little dull. Sometimes the outer layers peel off, revealing fresh white bark beneath, but you can help it along by giving it a bit of a scrub with slightly soapy water. This is a particularly good idea come winter, when you really want the bark to gleam.

Make sure you choose a tree that isn't going to outgrow the available space. Silver birches look terrible when pruned; they really need to be left just to grow. If your space is restricted, look for a smaller-growing cultivar such as *B. u. var. jacquemontii* 'Moonbeam'.

Hornbeam

Carpinus betulus

Situation:	Full sun or partial shade
Hardiness:	Hardy (USDA zone 8)
Soil type:	Fairly well drained
Height:	23 m/75 ft if left unpruned
Spread:	18 m/59 ft if left unpruned
Propagation:	Sow seed in autumn
Planting:	Plant out in autumn
Flowering period:	Catkins in spring
Toxicity:	Non-toxic

Hornbeam is a wonderful hedging plant for a night-time garden. It provides privacy and creates a sheltered environment where scents can linger long into the evening. It has similar-sized and shaped leaves to beech and, like beech, it is deciduous and will cling onto its leaves over winter if it is trimmed back regularly. The spring leaves are a pale, yellowy green; the summer leaves are mid-green; and the winter leaves are mid-brown, unlike the flashy glowing copper of winter beech leaves. Hornbeam's leaves are still very attractive – just subtler.

Hornbeam is a better choice than beech in moister, heavier soils. It will also stand much colder conditions than beech, so it is the best choice if you are planting in a frost pocket. Make a trench the length of your hedge and mix in lots of organic matter before backfilling. Plant bare-rooted plants in winter, spacing them 45 cm /18 in apart. For a really thick, dense hedge, plant a second, staggered row about 40 cm/15 in behind the first. Hornbeam is also worth considering as a pleached hedge. This is essentially a 'hedge on stilts'; it is a great way of creating a formal structure that can be underplanted with more informal planting. Prune in late summer for the best leaf retention through winter.

Kashmir Rowan

Sorbus cashmiriana

Situation:	Full sun or partial shade
Hardiness:	Hardy (USDA zone 8)
Soil type:	Moist, well drained, slightly alkaline
Height:	7 m /23 ft
Spread:	6 m/19 ft 6 in
Propagation:	Sow seed in autumn
Planting:	Plant in autumn
Flowering period:	Spring
Toxicity:	Non-toxic

The Kashmir rowan is a beautiful small tree that bears pink blossom in spring and berries in summer and autumn. While the common rowan's berries are bright red, those of *Sorbus cashmiriana* are large and pure white. They hang from fine, yellow-red stems in big, heavy bunches and show up, pure and pearly, in low light.

Although it eventually reaches quite a good size, this is a slow-growing tree and is a lovely choice for a small garden. Common rowans were traditionally planted outside front doors to ward away witches, and I see no reason why the same shouldn't go for the Kashmir rowan. In fact, I have one outside my own front door. It gradually spreads to become almost as wide as it is tall, and its leaves turn golden in autumn.

This tree does well in a range of soil conditions, although it seems to prefer a slightly alkaline soil, so avoid it if your soil is of the rhododendron-nurturing acid type. It is not as tough as the common rowan, so don't plant it in a frost pocket. Ideally, it needs sun and shelter from wind, although it will do pretty well in partial shade, too. Keep the soil moist and rich by mulching the roots with a thick layer of organic matter each year in autumn or spring.

Korean Fir

Abies koreana

Situation:	Full sun or partial shade
Hardiness:	Hardy (USDA zone 8)
Soil type:	Moist, well drained, slightly acidic
Height:	6 m/19 ft 6 in
Spread:	3 m/9 ft 9 in
Propagation:	Sow seed in autumn
Planting:	Plant out in autumn
Flowering period:	Cones in late spring
Toxicity:	Non-toxic

Most conifers either grow too large for the average garden or stay squat and tiny and just look silly. *Abies koreana* finds the happy middle ground between the two. It grows extremely slowly, but has a strong presence and stature, and could certainly not be called a dwarf conifer. It earns its place in the evening garden partly because of its excellent silhouette but also thanks to its needles. These are bright green on top with silver undersides. Because of their upward-pointing habit, the undersides are most beautifully revealed, giving the whole plant a silvery-blue sheen. The cultivar 'Silberlocke' has curved, slightly twisted needles that reveal the whole of their underside. This makes the plant even more silvery and even better suited to a moonlit garden.

In spring and into early summer, impressive violet-blue, upward-pointing cones are produced all over the branches. These hold fast all through the year, gradually turning brown as autumn approaches.

This is a spreading tree that really can't be pruned to fit a space. Any attempt at pruning will make it look extremely awkward, so choose a spot where it can spread out and achieve its full, majestic form. Ideally, you should plant it in full sun, but it can take some shade.

Plum

Prunus domestica

Situation:	Full sun
Hardiness:	Hardy (USDA zone 8)
Soil type:	Moist, well drained
Height:	Up to 9m/ 29 ft 6 in, depending on rootstock
Spread:	Up to 7 m/23 ft, depending on rootstock
Propagation:	Propagation can be from cuttings in summer, but plants grown on their own rootstock will grow very large and it is better to buy a grafted variety
Planting:	Plant in autumn
Flowering period:	Spring
Fruiting period:	Late summer to autumn
Toxicity:	Non-toxic

Like apple trees, plum trees bear blossom in spring and fruits in summer. They are attractive trees and within a few years bring an air of maturity to a garden and will provide a craggy silhouette against which to grow night-scented plants.

Plum blossom appears fairly early in the year, so there is always the possibility that it will be hit by a late frost. To guard against this, it is important to plant your tree in a sunny, sheltered spot and to avoid any frost pockets – areas such as dips in the ground or the base of slopes where frost settles and lingers. Plant into rich soil that doesn't get waterlogged; plums particularly resent sitting in water.

Plum trees can grow large, so choose one grown on a dwarfing rootstock such as 'Pixy' or 'St Julien A'. They also have a bit of a reputation as biennial bearers, meaning that they produce lots of fruit one year and none the next. That's because the plant exhausts itself ripening its huge crop and doesn't manage to make the following year's flower buds. To prevent this from happening, thin out the fruits when they first form and again at the end of early summer, aiming for an eventual spacing of 5 cm/2 in between fruits. 'Victoria' is one of the most popular varieties of plum as it is self-fertile and the fruits are delicious. 'Oullin's Gage' is another good, self-fertile variety.

Redbud

Cercis canadensis 'Forest Pansy'

Situation:	Full sun or partial shade
Hardiness:	Hardy (USDA zone 8)
Soil type:	Fairly moist with good drainage
Height:	9 m/29 ft 6. in
Spread:	9 m/29 ft 6. in
Propagation:	By layering in spring or from cuttings in summer
Planting:	Plant in spring
Flowering period:	Spring
Toxicity:	Mildly toxic

This deep purple leaved tree is a real beauty. It is yet another plant for adding depth of colour to a white scheme or simply for providing a dark background to show off a white scheme at its best. In spring, before the leaves come out, it produces purple or pink pea-like flowers. On a mature plant these can make an impressive show, but the plant's main feature is its heart-shaped leaves, which taper off into elegant, slender tips. They are darkest purple and glossy when they emerge, and turn a slightly duller reddish-green in summer. They then make up for this dullness by becoming a myriad of reds and golden yellows in autumn, often from the inside of the tree outwards, which creates the impression that the tree is being lit up from within.

Planting one of these small, multi-stemmed trees is perhaps the best way of getting really spectacular autumn foliage into a small garden. They look a little awkward as youngsters, but over the years they slowly grow into themselves. You can plant them against a wall or at the back of a border, but they look particularly good planted where they will have the autumn evening sun behind them. Then the coloured leaves light up like stained glass. Quite amazing!

Smoke Bush

Cotinus coggygria 'Royal Purple'

Situation:	Full sun or partial shade
Hardiness:	Hardy (USDA zone 8)
Soil type:	Fairly moist with good drainage
Height:	4 m/13 ft
Spread:	4 m/13 ft
Propagation:	By layering in spring or from cuttings in summer
Planting:	Plant in autumn
Flowering period:	Late summer
Toxicity:	Non-toxic

Cotinus coggygria 'Royal Purple' may seem a brooding shrub, but it is extremely useful. Its round leaves are dark purple and provide the perfect foil for all sorts of different-coloured flowers. They tone well with deep red roses and purple verbenas, making the colours of these look richer and deeper. They also provide a strong contrast to pale colours and acid greens. A pale pastel or white evening planting needs a darker accent in its midst to give it a bit of backbone, and cotinus is the perfect plant for this.

Cotinus is an extremely common shrub, so it's easy to think of it as not very special, but in fact it possesses some wonderful subtleties. When the leaves first emerge, they have a silky grey sheen; when they open, their midribs are a vibrant pink that sparks the purple foliage into life and prevents it becoming too sombre. In autumn, the leaves turn scarlet and pink before they fall.

Cotinus is often commonly known as the smoke bush because of its haze of flowers produced in late summer. If you want these, you should let the plant grow naturally, only pruning the oldest wood lightly. But if you want the largest, most impressive foliage, you should prune established plants right to the ground each spring.

Snowy Mespilus

Amelanchier × *lamarckii*

Situation:	Full sun or partial shade
Hardiness:	Hardy (USDA zone 8)
Soil type:	Acid, moist, well drained
Height:	6 m/19 ft 6 in
Spread:	3 m/9 ft 9 in
Propagation:	Sow seed in autumn
Planting:	Plant out in autumn
Flowering period:	Spring
Toxicity:	Non-toxic

While the pinnacle of sitting-out in the evening is obviously the summer, when the breezes are warm and night-scented plants are in full flood, it is good to have palely visible plants in the garden at other times of the year, too. Amelanchier is a beautiful white-flowered plant for early spring. It becomes so smothered in white flowers that it has the rather lovely common name of snowy mespilus. This is a plant that works hard for its place in the garden for most of the year, which makes it the perfect choice for a small garden. In spring there's that mass of white flowers; in summer it forms red, edible berries; and in autumn the foliage turns an impressive orange and red. In winter the plant isn't quite so spectacular, but it does have smooth, tactile, grey bark that looks good when the leaves have fallen.

The berries (hence its other common name, June berry) are edible, tasty, juicy and fruity with a hint of almond. Unfortunately, birds love them, too, so you'll need to net the tree if you want to be sure of getting them before the birds. If this is too much trouble, just be philosophical about it and view the berries as a boon for your birds.

Amelanchier prefers a moist, acid soil, but will tolerate a little dryness once it is really well established. It makes a small tree or a large, multi-stemmed shrub.

Weeping Pear

Pyrus salicifolia 'Pendula'

Situation:	Full sun
Hardiness:	Hardy (USDA zone 8)
Soil type:	Any
Height:	5 m/16 ft 4 in
Spread:	4 m/13 ft
Propagation:	From grafts in winter
Planting:	Plant in autumn
Flowering period:	Spring
Toxicity:	Non-toxic

With its sweeping, pendulous stems, weeping pear provides a dramatic backdrop and its silvery leaves that glint in the moonlight make it a must for the night-time garden. It's a great tree for small gardens, reaching only 5 m/16 ft 4 in in height, but it does like to spread out, becoming almost as wide as it is tall. Its main charm, though, lies in those stems. They sweep down then curve upwards at the ends, as if they have changed their mind halfway. They bear white flowers in early summer.

This is a tough plant and will grow well in a range of soil conditions, including very dry and stony soil. It also takes seaside conditions in its stride and is drought-tolerant. But the one thing it won't tolerate is wet soil.

When it comes to pruning, you have two alternatives. Either plant it somewhere it can really spread and don't prune at all; just let it all hang out and develop that beautiful swooping structure. Alternatively, prune it each year into a huge lollipop shape, which looks better than it sounds. The result is a formal shape but with a lovely soft edge. Pruning the weeping pear like this means it can even be grown in smaller gardens or it can be used as a recurring silvery accent plant throughout the garden. Prune in midsummer.

Winter-flowering Cherry

Prunus × *subhirtella* 'Autumnalis'

Situation:	Full sun
Hardiness:	Hardy (USDA zone 8)
Soil type:	Moist, well drained
Height:	8 m/26 ft
Spread:	8 m/26 ft
Propagation:	From cuttings in early summer
Planting:	Plant in autumn
Flowering period:	Late autumn to early spring
Toxicity:	Mildly toxic

We think of ornamental cherries as producing a vast, hugely impressive flurry of blossom in spring, making previously naked trees look as though they are covered in candyfloss. *Prunus x subhirtella* 'Autumnalis' isn't like that. It is an ornamental cherry that blooms intermittently all winter long, only taking the occasional break when the weather is particularly chilly. So don't expect the same floral fireworks you would get from a spring-flowering cherry. This is a far more subtle creature, but it's a truly delightful plant and almost guarantees that you will have something pale and ghostly blooming away in your garden throughout winter. For a really pretty pale effect, grow some snowdrops around the base.

This tree works hard for most of the year. There's the winter blossom and then in spring the new growth is a pretty bronze colour. In autumn, the leaves turn orange and gold. Its only boring season is summer, but then there's so much else going on in the garden that you are unlikely to notice. It is a fairly compact tree and doesn't cast heavy shade, so both these qualities make it great for the smaller garden. Because of its open, light habit, you could easily grow a clematis or other small climber through its branches to make the tree earn its keep during summer, too.

Yew

Taxus baccata

Situation:	Full sun to full shade
Hardiness:	Hardy (USDA zone 8)
Soil type:	Moist, well drained
Height:	Up to 20 m/65 ft 6 in if left unpruned (usually grown as a hedge or topiary)
Spread:	Up to 10 m/32 ft 9 in if left unpruned
Propagation:	Sow seed in autumn or take cuttings in late summer
Planting:	Plant in autumn
Flowering period:	Cones in spring, berries in late summer
Toxicity:	Almost all parts are toxic

All the best floral displays need a good backdrop and there's none better than yew. It will give you a dense, dark, night-time backdrop for a pale, silvery planting.

Yew has small, fine-textured leaves of the deepest green and can be used a dense hedge or as fabulously tactile topiary. Both of these will set off those delicate, pale, night-time beauties to perfection. It is as though the yew is lending the garden the solidity it needs to counterbalance the fripperies. As an autumn and winter bonus, it produces bright red berries, which birds love.

Yew isn't the fastest-growing hedging plant, but neither is it as slow as many imagine. The density of its texture makes it worth waiting for. It is also incredibly long-lived: any yew hedge you plant could last a couple of hundred years. So it's worth taking care and making sure that the ground is well prepared when you plant it. Dig out a trench and backfill it with garden compost mixed into the soil, then tread the soil down well. Use a line and pegs to lay out your hedge, and position the plants 45 cm/18 in apart. For a thicker hedge, plant a double row and stagger them.

Be warned that almost all parts of the plant are poisonous.

Index

A
Abies koreana 204-5
Allium giganteum 138-9
Amelanchier × *lamarckii* 212-3
angel's trumpet 80-1
Anthemis cupaniana 168-9
apples 182-3
arbours 23
Argyranthemum frutescens 148-9
arum lily 130-1

B
balconies 20-2
bamboo, black 23, 188-9
bamboo, heavenly 23, 196-7
barbecues 24, 50, 66-9
bats 71-2
bay tree 184-5
beech 186-7
Betula utilis subsp. *jacquemontii* 198-9
bistro lights 40, 51
black bamboo 188-9
bonfire night 54-5
boundaries 27
Brompton stock 114-5
Brugmansia suaveolens 35, 80-1
bunting 66

C
cabbage palm 190-1
calmondins 82-3
cameras for wildlife 75
camping 60-3
campion, white 34
candlelight 24, 38-40
canopies 22, 51
Carpinus betulus 200-1
Cercis canadensis 'Forest Pansy' 208-9
Cestrum nocturnum 110-1
chamomile, Sicilian 168-9
cherry pie (heliotrope) 92-3
cherry, winter-flowering 216-7
chicken, barbecue 69
Choisya ternata 51, 152-3
Christmas rose 132-3
Chusan palm 192-3
citrus 82-3
clematis 134-5
Clematis Montana 134-5
colour 9, 28-31
coneflower, purple 158-9
contemplation 22-3
Convallaria majalis 146-7
Cordyline australis 20, 27, 51, 190-1
Cotinus coggygria 'Royal Purple' 210-1
crab apple 194-5

D
dame's rocket 84-5
daylily 86-7
decks 50
design
   colour 28-31
existing plants 10
lighting 38-43
planning 10, 15
scent 34-5
space 27
styles 17-24
usage considerations 15
water 45
Dianthus 35, 118-9
Digitalis purpurea f. *albiflora* 136-7

E
Echinacea purpurea 32-3, 158-9
electric lighting 42-3
enclosure 27
entertaining 50-69
Epiphyllum oxypetalum 120-1
evening primrose 34, 51, 71, 88-9

F
Fagus sylvatica 186-7
fairy lights 40, 51
family gardens 24
fir, Korean 204-5
fire pits 50, 55
fireworks 55
flowering tobacco 90-1
foliage 31
footprint tunnel 74
four o'clock plant 104-5
foxglove 136-7
front gardens 17-9
furniture 50

G

Galanthus nivalis 174-5
games 62
gazebos 50
Geranium pratense 150-1
giant allum 138-9
glow-worms 73
Gonospermum ptarmiciflorum 170-1

H

hammocks 24
hanging baskets 22
heavenly bamboo 196-7
hedgehogs 70
hedges 27, 31
heliotrope 20, 92-3
Heliotropium arborescens 92-3
Helleborus niger 132-3
Hemerocallis 51, 86-7
Hesperis matronalis 84-5
Himalayan birch 198-9
honeysuckle 18, 35, 71, 94-5, 178-9
hornbeam 200-1
hydrangeas 18, 172-3

I

Ipomoea alba 108-9
irrigation systems 20

J

Japanese wisteria 18, 96-7
jasmine 18, 34, 35, 98-9
jessamine, night-blooming 110-1

K

Kashmir rowan 202-3
Korean fir 204-5

L

lamb's ear 'silver carpet' 140-1
landscaping 10
Laurus nobilis 184-5
Lavandula angustifolia 142-3
lavender 142-3
lavender cotton 144-5
lawns 24, 50
lemons 82-3
lighting 18, 23, 24, 38-43, 51
lilies 20, 34, 35, 100-3
Lilium regale 100-3
lily of the valley 146-7
limes 82-3
log piles 72
Lonicera fragrantissima 178-9
Lonicera japonica 94-5

M

maintenance time 15
Malus × *zumi* 'Golden Hornet' 194-5
Malus domestica 182-3
marguerite daisy 148-9
marvel-of-Peru 104-5
Matthiola bicorni subsp. *bicornis* 34, 114-5
Matthiola incana 114-5
meadow cranesbill 150-1
meteors 56, 59
Mexican orange blossom 152-3
Mirabilis jalapa 20, 104-5
mock orange 18, 154-5
moon-gazing party 56-9
'moon-gazing pond' 45
moonflower 108-9
moth lure 74
moths 71, 74

N

Nandina domestica 23, 196-7
Nepeta 'Six Hills Giant' 29
Nicotiana sylvestris 90-1
night-blooming jessamine 110-1
night scented phlox 112-3
night-scented stock 20, 34, 114-5

O

Oenothera biennis 88-9

P

Paeonia 'Claire de Lune' 156-7
parties 50-9, 64-7
patios 50
pear, weeping 214-5
peonies 156-7
pergolas 22, 23, 35
petunias 22, 116-7
Philadelphus 18, 154-5
phlox, night scented 112-3
Phyllostachys nigra 188-9
pinks, 'Mrs Sinkins' 118-9
pizza ovens 24, 50
plums 206-7
Polianthes tuberosa 126-7
pollinators 34
ponds 44-5
pots and containers 20, 35
privacy 22, 27, 51
privet hedge 31
Prunus × *subhirtella* 'Autumnalis' 216-7
Prunus domestica 206-7
purple coneflower 158-9
purple top 160-1
Pyrus salicifolia 'Pendula' 214-5

Q
queen of the night 120-1

R
redbud 208-9
rosemary 164-5
roses 35, 162-3
rowan, Kashmir 202-3

S
sage 166-7
Salvia officinalis 166-7
sandpits 24
Santolina chamaecyparissus 144-5
Saponaria officinalis 122-3
scent 9, 34-5
seating 20, 23, 24, 50-1
Sicilian chamomile 168-9
Silene alba 34
silver feather 170-1
Sissinghurst Castle Garden, Kent 5
small gardens 20-2
smoke bush 210-1
smores 55
snowdrops 174-5
snowy mespilus 212-3
soapwort 122-3
Sorbus cashmiriana 202-3
sounds 9, 22, 23, 45
Stachys byzantina 'Silver Carpet' 140-1
star-gazing party 56-9
star jasmine 124-5
stock, night-scented 114-5
sweet rocket 71, 84-5

T
Taxus baccata 218-9
telescopes 56

theatre night 64-5
tobacco, flowering 71, 90-1
Trachelospermum jasminoides 51, 124-5
Trachycarpus fortunei 20, 27, 51, 192-3
tuberose 126-7
tulips 30, 176-7

V
verandas 22
Verbena bonariensis 31, 160-1
water
  design 45
  features 22, 23, 45
  pots 20
  sounds 9, 22, 23, 45

W
weeping pear 214-5
white campion 34
wildlife 7, 9, 42, 45, 70-5
wind chimes 23
winter-flowering cherry 216-7
winter honeysuckle 18, 178-9
Wisteria floribunda 18, 96-7

Y
yew 31, 218-9

Z
Zaluzianskya ovata 20, 112-3
Zantedeschia aethiopica 130-1

G

Galanthus nivalis 174-5
games 62
gazebos 50
Geranium pratense 150-1
giant allum 138-9
glow-worms 73
Gonospermum ptarmiciflorum 170-1

H

hammocks 24
hanging baskets 22
heavenly bamboo 196-7
hedgehogs 70
hedges 27, 31
heliotrope 20, 92-3
Heliotropium arborescens 92-3
Helleborus niger 132-3
Hemerocallis 51, 86-7
Hesperis matronalis 84-5
Himalayan birch 198-9
honeysuckle 18, 35, 71, 94-5, 178-9
hornbeam 200-1
hydrangeas 18, 172-3

I

Ipomoea alba 108-9
irrigation systems 20

J

Japanese wisteria 18, 96-7
jasmine 18, 34, 35, 98-9
jessamine, night-blooming 110-1

K

Kashmir rowan 202-3
Korean fir 204-5

L

lamb's ear 'silver carpet' 140-1
landscaping 10
Laurus nobilis 184-5
Lavandula angustifolia 142-3
lavender 142-3
lavender cotton 144-5
lawns 24, 50
lemons 82-3
lighting 18, 23, 24, 38-43, 51
lilies 20, 34, 35, 100-3
Lilium regale 100-3
lily of the valley 146-7
limes 82-3
log piles 72
Lonicera fragrantissima 178-9
Lonicera japonica 94-5

M

maintenance time 15
Malus × *zumi* 'Golden Hornet' 194-5
Malus domestica 182-3
marguerite daisy 148-9
marvel-of-Peru 104-5
Matthiola bicorni subsp. *bicornis* 34, 114-5
Matthiola incana 114-5
meadow cranesbill 150-1
meteors 56, 59
Mexican orange blossom 152-3
Mirabilis jalapa 20, 104-5
mock orange 18, 154-5
moon-gazing party 56-9
'moon-gazing pond' 45
moonflower 108-9
moth lure 74
moths 71, 74

N

Nandina domestica 23, 196-7
Nepeta 'Six Hills Giant' 29
Nicotiana sylvestris 90-1
night-blooming jessamine 110-1
night scented phlox 112-3
night-scented stock 20, 34, 114-5

O

Oenothera biennis 88-9

P

Paeonia 'Claire de Lune' 156-7
parties 50-9, 64-7
patios 50
pear, weeping 214-5
peonies 156-7
pergolas 22, 23, 35
petunias 22, 116-7
Philadelphus 18, 154-5
phlox, night scented 112-3
Phyllostachys nigra 188-9
pinks, 'Mrs Sinkins' 118-9
pizza ovens 24, 50
plums 206-7
Polianthes tuberosa 126-7
pollinators 34
ponds 44-5
pots and containers 20, 35
privacy 22, 27, 51
privet hedge 31
Prunus × *subhirtella* 'Autumnalis' 216-7
Prunus domestica 206-7
purple coneflower 158-9
purple top 160-1
Pyrus salicifolia 'Pendula' 214-5

Q
queen of the night 120-1

R
redbud 208-9
rosemary 164-5
roses 35, 162-3
rowan, Kashmir 202-3

S
sage 166-7
Salvia officinalis 166-7
sandpits 24
Santolina chamaecyparissus 144-5
Saponaria officinalis 122-3
scent 9, 34-5
seating 20, 23, 24, 50-1
Sicilian chamomile 168-9
Silene alba 34
silver feather 170-1
Sissinghurst Castle Garden, Kent 5
small gardens 20-2
smoke bush 210-1
smores 55
snowdrops 174-5
snowy mespilus 212-3
soapwort 122-3
Sorbus cashmiriana 202-3
sounds 9, 22, 23, 45
Stachys byzantina 'Silver Carpet' 140-1
star-gazing party 56-9
star jasmine 124-5
stock, night-scented 114-5
sweet rocket 71, 84-5

T
Taxus baccata 218-9
telescopes 56

theatre night 64-5
tobacco, flowering 71, 90-1
Trachelospermum jasminoides 51, 124-5
Trachycarpus fortunei 20, 27, 51, 192-3
tuberose 126-7
tulips 30, 176-7

V
verandas 22
Verbena bonariensis 31, 160-1
water
  design 45
  features 22, 23, 45
  pots 20
  sounds 9, 22, 23, 45

W
weeping pear 214-5
white campion 34
wildlife 7, 9, 42, 45, 70-5
wind chimes 23
winter-flowering cherry 216-7
winter honeysuckle 18, 178-9
Wisteria floribunda 18, 96-7

Y
yew 31, 218-9

Z
Zaluzianskya ovata 20, 112-3
Zantedeschia aethiopica 130-1

PICTURE CREDITS

Alamy / Simon Clairac 120; / Elizabeth Whiting & Associates 102–103; / John Glover 36-37 / The Garden Picture Library 101; / Florapix 99 / Larina Elena 14 / mauritius images GmbH 38 / Botany vision 208;

GAP Photos / Pernilla Bergdahl 160; / Adrian Bloom 173; / Richard Bloom 211; / Christina Bollen 206; / Mark Bolton 151, 183, 194; / Elke Borkowski 6; / Lynne Brotchie 117; / Jonathan Buckley 85, 125; / Jonathan Buckley / Design: Helen Yemm 78; / Leigh Clapp 82; / Heather Edwards 106–107 / John Glover 26, 119, 190; / Jerry Harpur / Design: Simon Fraser 184; / Jerry Harpur / Design: Ulf Nordfjell 21 / Jerry Harpur / Design: Bob Parker and Greg Kowalczuk 41; / Marcus Harpur 81, 115 (inset top), 169, 189; / Marcus Harpur / Design: Jason Payne 193; / Charles Hawes 115 (main), 174; / Martin Hughes-Jones 123, 155 167; / Janet Johnson 16; / Lynn Keddie 218; / Geoff Kidd 105, 152; / Fiona Lea 89; / Zara Napier 163 (left inset), 180; / Clive Nichols 30, 138, 145, 167; / Clive Nichols / Design: Claire Mee 43; / Clive Nichols / Location: Lower Hall, Shropshire 163 (main); / Howard Rice 92, 109, 217; / Maayke de Ridder / Design: Alexandre Thomas 177; / S & Oß 130; / J S Sira 115 (inset bottom), 113, 170, 203; / Graham Strong 133; / Maddie Thornhill 97; / Visions 87, 157; / Juliette Wade 8, 163 (right inset), 187; / Rob Whitworth 237; / Rob Whitworth / Design: Clare Agnew 200; / Rob Whitworth / Location: RHS Gardens Wisley 199; / Dave Zubraski 135; 149;

Getty / R A Kearton 95 / Flashpop 48, 52-53 / Nomadnes 63 / Anchiy 68 / PeopleImages 57;

© MMGI / Marianne Majerus / Appletrees / Kath Butcher 11;

Clive Nichols / 29, 44;

Photolibrary / Peter Baistow 5; / Lynne Brotchie 128; / Paroli Galperti 111; / Clive Nichols 32–33; / Harley Seaway 91; / Paul Viant 25;

The Garden Collection / Torie Chugg 179; / Derek Harris 146, 196; / Andrew Lawson 164, 205 / Gary Rogers 141; / Derek St Romaine 158; / Nicola Stocken Tomkins 212, 214

ABOUT THE AUTHOR

Lia Leendertz is a garden and food writer, and the presenter of the *As the Season Turns* podcast. She is the author of the bestselling annual book *The Almanac: A Seasonal Guide*. Lia has a town garden and she loves to spend time in it during the evenings.

First published in 2011 by
Pavilion
An imprint of HarperCollins*Publishers* Ltd
1 London Bridge Street
London SE1 9GF

www.harpercollins.co.uk

HarperCollins*Publishers*
Macken House
39/40 Mayor Street Upper
Dublin 1
D01 C9W8
Ireland

10 9 8 7 6 5 4 3 2 1

This edition first published in Great Britain by Pavilion
An imprint of HarperCollins*Publishers* 2026

Copyright © Pavilion 2011, 2026
Text © Lia Leendertz 2011, 2026
Photography © picture credits on page 223

Lia Leendertz asserts the moral right to be identified as the author of this work. A catalogue record of this book is available from the British Library.

ISBN 978-0-00-872505-1

For the first edition:

Commissioning Editor: Emily Preece-Morrison
Cover Design and Concept: Georgina Hewitt
Layout: Louise Leffler
Picture Research: Jenny Faithfull
Editors: Hilary Mandleberg, Nicola Hodgson
Illustrations: Karolin Schnoor
Indexer: Sandra Shotter

This edition credits:

Publishing Directior: Laura Russell
Managing Editor: Shamar Gunning
Editorial Assistant: Daisy Gudmunsen
Managing Designer: Lily Wilson
Layout Designer: James Boast
Proofreader: Molly Price
Indexer: Ruth Ellis
Production Controller: Emma Hatlen

Printed and bound by Papercraft in Malaysia

All rights reserved. No part of this publication may be reproduced, stored in a retrieval system, or transmitted, in any form or by any means, electronic, mechanical, photocopying, recording or otherwise, without the prior written permission of the publishers.

Without limiting the author's and publisher's exclusive rights, any unauthorised use of this publication to train generative artificial intelligence (AI) technologies is expressly prohibited. HarperCollins also exercise their rights under Article 4(3) of the Digital Single Market Directive 2019/790 and expressly reserve this publication from the text and data mining exception.

WHEN USING KITCHEN APPLIANCES PLEASE ALWAYS FOLLOW THE MANUFACTURER'S INSTRUCTIONS.

ALWAYS CONSULT AN ELECTRICAN TO ENSURE WIRING IS CORRECTLY ROUTED AND INSTALLED.